Culinary greetings from

HOLLAND AMERICA LINE

HOLLAND AMERICA LINE

APPETIZERS

VOLUME IV
Culinary Signature Collection

RUDI SODAMIN

RIZZOLI
NEW YORK

First published in the United States of America in 2012
by Rizzoli International Publications, Inc.
300 Park Avenue South
New York, NY 10010
www.rizzoliusa.com

2012 2013 2014 2015 / 10 9 8 7 6 5 4 3 2 1

ISBN-13: 978-0-8478-3819-6

Library of Congress Control Number: 2012937147

Design by Susi Oberhelman

Distributed in the U.S. trade by Random House, New York

Printed in China

Page 1: Chinese Beef Saté with Asian Broccoli Slaw (pages 48–49)
Page 2: Polenta with Caponata and Crisp Red Onions (pages 156–157)
Page 5: Seafood Brioche (pages 132–133)
Page 6: Philippine Pork Spring Rolls with Spicy Asian Slaw (pages 66–67)
Page 8: Chicken and Mushroom Ragoût in Vol-au-Vent (pages 144–145)

DEDICATION

To the culinary artists of tomorrow

This is a book entirely about beginnings. Appetizers set the stage for the excitement of what's to come. It seemed only fitting, then, to dedicate this volume to the young men and women at the beginning of their careers currently pursuing their education in culinary schools and rising in the ranks in restaurant kitchens and ships' galleys throughout the world.

The life of a young chef is not an easy one: The hours are long, the pay in the beginning is modest, and the physical demands are intense. Yet every chef I've ever met does what he or she does for a living because they cannot imagine themselves being truly happy doing anything else. The desire to discover, create, nourish people body and soul, and continually seek fresh inspiration is the passion behind the profession.

These young culinarians are the tastemakers of tomorrow, and with this dedication I applaud their commitment and wish for them the same abundant measure of success and satisfaction I have enjoyed since I donned my first toque.

CONTENTS

L O O K I N G

At Holland America Line one of our key ingredients to success is looking forward. Whether it's to predict our guests' every need and desire, to seek out new destinations, or to deliver a cutting-edge culinary experience, we continually look to the future to set new standards of excellence for creating once-in-a-lifetime experiences for guests.

It is this forward-thinking mind-set that has made Holland America Line a leader in premium cruising. The powerful momentum derived from enthusiastically embracing innovation is tremendously exciting and brings vitality to everything we do.

Today, our fleet of fifteen ships offers more than 500 cruises to 350 ports in over 100 countries, territories, and dependencies. Two- to 115-day itineraries visit all seven continents featuring Antarctica, South America, Australia and New Zealand, and Asia Voyages; a Grand World Voyage; and sailings to ports in the Caribbean, Alaska, Hawaii, Canada and New England, Europe, and the Panama Canal. Each year, the list of travel options for our guests' pleasure and adventure grows.

Yet equally important is what our guests experience when traveling on board one of our ships. From the magnificent décor and stellar service to our engaging activities, each trip is carefully orchestrated to build a sense of excitement and anticipation for what is next.

Our approach to generating this anticipation is well illustrated by the philosophy Master Chef Rudi Sodamin brings to our dining programs. Guided by his world-famous culinary theatricality, Master Chef Rudi's innovative menus begin with an attention-getting arrangement of brilliant flavor notes and build to a resounding crescendo.

As the curtain rises, it all starts with the appetizers. Like the opening scene of a play, or the first chapter of a page-turner book, appetizers must immediately engage the attention of the audience, drawing them into the experience, without giving away too much all

F O R W A R D

at once. Chef Rudi suggests that "a wonderful meal is like a great romance: It starts with beauty, intrigue, and teasing promises of the good things to come."

Accordingly, Master Chef Rudi creates appetizers for Holland America Line menus that are impressively provocative—stimulating not only the appetite but all the senses with artful presentations, enticing aromas, and tantalizing flavors. This book is devoted exclusively to the art of creating appetizers that will have the same affect on your guests as they do on ours—your guests will feel that they have been treated to something truly special and will expect that after such a spectacular start the entire event will be filled with pleasure.

From our extraordinary database of signature Holland America Line recipes, Master Chef Rudi has selected a dynamic collection of appetizers that have been adapted and scaled for the home cook. Additionally, you'll find sensational recipes from the other internationally celebrated members of the Holland America Line Culinary Council—Chefs Jonnie Boer, David Burke, Marcus Samuelsson, Charlie Trotter, and Jacques Torres.

At Holland America Line, we thoroughly immerse ourselves in carefully planning, staging, and executing every aspect of our guests' journeys so their experience from start to finish exceeds their expectations. In short, we look forward so our guests will take great pleasure in looking back. You can bring this same excitement to your dining events at home by setting the stage with recipes from this wonderful collection in the new volume of the Culinary Signature Collection.

As always, I wish you happy cooking and pleasurable dining. We look forward to welcoming you aboard.

STEIN KRUSE
President and Chief Executive Officer

MASTER CHEF RUDI SODAMIN'S PLEASURES OF THE TABLE

I AM NOT SURE HOW MUCH PRAISE I CAN HEAP UPON Chef/Legend Rudi Sodamin without him turning completely red in the face, but I am going to try. I will start by saying that this is a brilliant book, simply astonishing in its breadth and depth. These recipes are perfect for both the home cook and the professional (indeed, I intend to steal a few!).

Chef Rudi not only brings a delicate sensuality to his preparations, but an easy-to-grasp precision that can only come from a seasoned veteran of the best of professional kitchens. The other amazing thing that will be discovered in these pages is a virtual trip around the world in terms of the variety and diversity of the offerings. This is perhaps because Chef Rudi has traveled countless times to every corner of the globe. I guess it never hurts to have pristine and classic culinary training and subsequently work for the iconic Holland America Line.

The greatest thing about Chef Rudi, though, is not just his worldwide perspective on great food or his exquisite technique in assembling his masterpieces, it's his sheer joy of being around people and sharing one of life's most important things—the pleasures of the table! One warms in his glow and feels his love the minute he starts talking about food. Rudi is a chef filled with exuberance, and it will be experienced with every recipe in this magnificent book. No wonder his motto is "What's cookin', good lookin'?"

Rudi—you're the best!

CHEF CHARLIE TROTTER

CHAPTER 1

ROLLS, WRAPS, AND FILLED BITES

Taking a cruise on Holland America Line is about celebrating life. It's about having new experiences. It's about indulging all of your senses. It's about surprises and discoveries. It's about feeling special and, most important, it's about having fun with people you love.

I chose to launch the Culinary Signature Collection's *Appetizers* with this delicious collection of rolls, wraps, and filled bites because they are pure fun—fun to make and fun to eat—and lend themselves to creativity in the kitchen. Think of these recipes as little wrapped gifts—there's no telling what's inside until you bite into it and experience the delightful burst of flavor inside.

The other thing I love about the collection of recipes in this chapter is that they reflect culinary traditions from around the globe—you'll find Asian, European, and Latin influences, and if you've ever taken one of our cruises to Alaska you'll especially appreciate the Halibut Quesadillas with Pico de Gallo and Guacamole. Every recipe in this chapter is one that has been highly requested for cocktail parties and special events aboard our ships.

While it was difficult to narrow down the selection of party favorites from our extensive list of most-requested rolls, wraps, and filled bites for this cookbook, it won't be difficult for you to make them. The key to enjoying the process of making these little flavor-packed gifts for your guests is to set all your ingredients out and do all the prep work in advance; then the recipes are simple to assemble—you can even enlist your guests to get wrapping, rolling, and filling together in the kitchen. It's all about the fun.

Smoked Duck and Vegetable Spring Rolls with Mandarin Orange Salad

MANDARIN ORANGE SALAD

2 clementines or Mandarin-type oranges, peel and pith removed and fruit cut into sections

¾ cup bean sprouts

2 tablespoons sliced scallion

2 teaspoons sesame oil

1 teaspoon sugar

¼ teaspoon salt

½ cup grated carrot

DUCK ROLLS

1 cup bean sprouts, tailed

1 ounce dried bean thread noodles (also called glass or cellophane noodles; optional), soaked in hot water for 30 minutes, drained, and cut into ½-inch pieces with a scissors

¼ cup finely minced red onion

2 medium scallions, white part plus 2 inches green, cut into thin strips

2 tablespoons chopped fresh cilantro

2 teaspoons fresh lime juice

1 teaspoon mirin (sweet Japanese rice wine)

10 thin Vietnamese rice paper rounds (*banh trang*), 8½ inches in diameter

4 to 6 ounces boneless smoked duck, cut into thin strips

1 large carrot, trimmed, peeled, and cut into thin strips

¾ cup very thinly sliced romaine lettuce (ribs removed)

¾ cup bottled or homemade Asian-style peanut dipping sauce (page 37)

¼ cup roasted peanuts, chopped

ny leftover cooked meat (ham, pork, turkey, or chicken) or even crabmeat or small shrimp can substitute for the duck in these delightful rice paper rolls, which are filled and served fresh rather than deep fried.

1. Make the Mandarin orange salad: In a small glass or ceramic bowl, toss all the salad ingredients with a rubber spatula until combined. Set aside.

2. Make the duck rolls: In a small bowl, combine the bean sprouts, bean thread noodles (if using), red onion, scallions, cilantro, lime juice, and mirin. Set aside.

3. Assemble the rolls: Pour 2 cups warm water into a large bowl. Place a sheet of plastic wrap on a work surface. One at a time, immerse a rice paper sheet in the warm water and let it stay there for 30 seconds. Quickly remove it and lay it flat on the plastic wrap (this will help the rice paper quickly become pliable).

4. Spoon a portion of the bean sprout mixture on the bottom third of the sheet. Top with some duck, carrot, and lettuce. With damp fingers and hands, fold the sides of the rice paper in and roll it up like a cylinder, using the plastic wrap to guide you. Transfer the roll to a plate and cover with more plastic wrap or a damp kitchen towel so it will stay moist as you fill the remaining rice paper wrappers. Don't stack the finished rolls or allow them to touch each other—they'll be very sticky. (The rolls can be prepared to this point up to three hours ahead at room temperature, covered with plastic wrap or a damp towel.)

5. To serve, slice each spring roll in half diagonally and place on plate, one half standing upright. With tongs, arrange some Mandarin salad behind the rolls. Drizzle with the peanut sauce and sprinkle with chopped peanuts.

NOTE | Vietnamese rice paper rounds come in various sizes. They're translucent and sport a crosshatch pattern from having been dried on bamboo trays. They are available in Asian grocery stores.

Spinach Phyllo Triangles

These universally loved spinach and cheese pastries are a variation of what appear on our Warm Greek Sampler plate. They can also be made larger, to serve with a salad for a light lunch. If you'd like, serve them with tzatziki sauce (see Grilled Lamb Kebabs with Tzatziki, page 34).

1. With your hands, in a kitchen towel, or in a strainer, squeeze the spinach until very dry. In a food processor, combine the spinach, parsley, dill, cheeses, lemon juice, garlic, and egg. Season with pepper. Process until smooth. Transfer to a bowl and stir in the pine nuts. Cover and refrigerate for 1 hour or up to 1 day.

2. Remove the phyllo stack from the box and lay it flat between two sheets of waxed paper or plastic wrap, then cover the stack with a very slightly damp towel. This will prevent the crumbling of yet-to-be-used phyllo sheets while you assemble the pastries.

3. Preheat the oven to 375°F. Line two baking sheets with parchment paper. On a work surface, arrange a phyllo sheet with a long side facing you and brush it lightly with melted butter. Cover with a second phyllo sheet and brush with butter again. With a pizza cutter or a chef's knife, cut the phyllo sheets crosswise into 6 equal strips (about 3 inches wide). (Alternatively, cut the sheets into 3 equal strips for larger pastries and fill with twice the amount of filling to make a total of 15 pastries.)

4. Working quickly with one strip at a time (keeping the others covered, if necessary), place a heaping teaspoon of the spinach mixture in the center of each strip about ½ inch from the end nearest you. Fold a corner across the filling and continue to fold, as if you were folding a flag, until the strip is all folded into a neat triangle. Brush both sides with melted butter and place seam side down and 1 inch apart on a prepared baking sheet. Repeat with the remaining phyllo sheets and filling, until you've made 30 pastries. (The pastries can be frozen at this point for 30 minutes on the baking sheet, then transferred to freezer bags and stored in the freezer for up to 1 month; do not thaw before baking for 30 to 40 minutes in a preheated 375°F oven.)

5. Bake the triangles in the middle of the oven until golden brown, about 20 minutes. Transfer to a rack and let cool slightly. Serve as a passed appetizer or arrange on plates with the arugula and halved cherry tomatoes as garnish.

YIELD: 30 PASTRIES

1 (10-ounce) package frozen chopped spinach, thawed

½ cup chopped fresh parsley

½ cup minced fresh dill

4 ounces cream cheese, softened

½ cup crumbled feta cheese

½ cup (4 ounces) farmers cheese or ricotta

2 tablespoons grated Parmesan cheese

2 teaspoons fresh lemon juice

½ teaspoon minced garlic

1 large egg, lightly beaten

Freshly ground black pepper

3 tablespoons chopped pine nuts, lightly toasted

10 (17-by-12-inch) phyllo sheets (8 ounces), thawed overnight in the refrigerator

½ cup (1 stick) unsalted butter, melted

4 ounces baby arugula (optional)

1 pint cherry tomatoes, halved (optional)

Halibut Quesadillas with Pico de Gallo and Guacamole

YIELD: 5 QUESADILLAS
(10 SERVINGS)

4 tablespoons olive oil

1 pound skinless halibut fillet, about 1 inch thick

Coarse sea salt and freshly ground black pepper

10 ounces cream cheese or creamy-style feta cheese, at room temperature

1 large red bell pepper, roasted (see Note), peeled, and diced; or 2 ounces roasted red peppers from a jar, diced

3 tablespoons chopped fresh cilantro, plus 10 sprigs for garnish

1½ tablespoons minced jalapeño pepper

1 teaspoon finely minced garlic

10 (6- to 8-inch) flour tortillas

1 cup (4 ounces) grated Monterey Jack cheese

4 medium tomatoes, seeded and diced

½ cup pitted, sliced black olives

1½ cups Pico de Gallo (page 155)

1 avocado, peeled and mashed

4 small limes, cut into wedges

1 cup sour cream

 his is like a fish taco to eat with a knife and fork—all the better for combining the various ingredients in each mouthful.

1. In a large heavy skillet, heat 2 tablespoons of the oil over medium-high heat. Sprinkle the halibut on both sides with salt and pepper and add it to the skillet. Cook one side until lightly browned, about 3 minutes. Gently flip the fish, lower the heat to medium, and cook for about 4 minutes, until the fish is opaque in the center and a thermometer inserted into the thickest part of the fish registers 135°F. Transfer the fish to a plate and let cool slightly before using.

2. Preheat the oven to 200°F. In a medium bowl, whip the cream cheese until fluffy. With a spatula, fold in the roasted pepper, cilantro, jalapeño, and garlic.

3. Lay two tortillas on a work surface and spread both evenly with some of the cream cheese mixture. With a fork, flake the halibut and scatter one fifth on one tortilla. Top with some of the Monterey Jack cheese, tomatoes, and olives. Invert the second prepared tortilla on top, creating a sandwich, and set aside. Repeat with the remaining tortillas.

4. Heat a nonstick skillet over medium heat and brush with some of the remaining oil. Place a quesadilla in the skillet and brush the top of it lightly with more oil. Cook, turning once, until the tortilla is slightly browned, 3 to 4 minutes per side. Transfer the quesadilla to a baking sheet and keep warm in the oven while cooking the remaining quesadillas.

NOTE | To roast red bell peppers: Working with one or two peppers at a time, place the peppers directly on the burner grate of a gas stove and char, turning them often with long tongs, until they are blackened on all sides. (Alternatively, roast them in a 500°F oven, stem end down, on a baking sheet until uniformly charred, 8 to 10 minutes.) When the peppers are charred, immediately remove them from the heat and place them in a heavy-duty brown-paper bag, close it tightly, and secure it with a clip or rubber band. Let the peppers steam in the bag for 10 minutes. When the peppers are cool enough to handle, peel off the charred skin and discard it; use a blunt knife to remove any bits of skin that adhere.

5. Add ½ cup of the pico de gallo to the mashed avocado and stir just until the guacamole is combined but still chunky. Season with salt and pepper and some of the lime juice (from 2 or 3 lime wedges).

6. To serve, cut each quesadilla into four pieces and place two pieces on each serving plate. Arrange the remaining pico de gallo, the guacamole, sour cream, and lime wedges around. Place a cilantro sprig on each plate and serve immediately.

Mexican Cornmeal Griddle Cakes with Avocado

Make these thin like a crêpe to contrast with the chunky avocado filling.

1. Make the avocado filling: In a glass or ceramic bowl, mix the avocado and scallions with a fork until well combined but with some chunks still visible. Fold in the tomatoes and lemon juice. Season with Tabasco sauce, salt, and pepper. Cover and refrigerate for 20 minutes.

2. Make the griddle cakes: In a large bowl, combine the flour, cornmeal, sugar, baking powder, and salt. In a medium bowl, whisk the buttermilk, eggs, and butter until smooth. Make a well in the dry ingredients; add the wet ingredients and beat until the batter is free of lumps. Cover with plastic wrap and let stand for 20 minutes.

3. Place a small skillet over medium heat. With a pastry brush, coat the pan with some oil. Using a small ladle, add only enough batter to the pan to coat the base with a thin layer, as if to make a 5- to 6-inch crêpe. When golden on the bottom (about 1 minute), flip the griddle cake and cook for just a few seconds more. Transfer the griddle cake to a plate and cover with a kitchen towel to keep warm. Repeat with the remaining batter, brushing the pan with oil before cooking and stacking the griddle cakes as you go.

4. To serve, spoon some of the avocado filling on one half of each griddle cake and fold the other half over. Divide the griddle cakes among warmed plates and serve with sour cream sprinkled with scallions on the side.

YIELD: 4 TO 6 SERVINGS

AVOCADO FILLING

1 large ripe avocado, cut in half lengthwise, peeled, pitted, and diced

8 scallions, finely chopped

2 ripe tomatoes, seeded and chopped

2 teaspoons fresh lemon juice

Green Tabasco sauce

Salt and freshly ground black pepper

GRIDDLE CAKES

½ cup all-purpose flour

⅓ cup yellow cornmeal

1 teaspoon sugar

¼ teaspoon baking powder

¼ teaspoon salt

1 cup buttermilk

2 large eggs

2 tablespoons unsalted butter, melted

2 tablespoons vegetable oil, plus more as needed

Sour cream, for garnish

Scallions, thinly sliced, for garnish

Chicken and Sun-Dried Tomato Roulade with Guava Dressing

YIELD: 4 TO 6 SERVINGS

GUAVA VINAIGRETTE

2 tablespoons canned guava nectar (see Notes)

1 tablespoon rice vinegar

2½ teaspoons sugar

1¼ teaspoons pasteurized egg white (see Notes)

Salt and freshly ground black pepper

⅓ cup vegetable oil

ROULADES

4 (6-ounce) boneless, skinless chicken breast halves

6 ounces feta cheese, preferably creamy French-style

¼ cup finely chopped sun-dried tomatoes (about 1 ounce)

3 tablespoons thinly sliced fresh basil

Salt and freshly ground black pepper

Flour for dredging

2 tablespoons olive oil

4 to 6 thin slices prosciutto

4 to 6 cherry tomatoes, quartered

1 cup frisée lettuce

8 to 12 kalamata olives

4 to 6 sprigs fresh thyme

These make-ahead roulades are served cold and are accompanied with an unusual, frothy dressing.

1. Make the guava vinaigrette: In a food processor or blender, combine guava nectar, vinegar, sugar, and egg white. Season with salt and pepper. Blend for 1 to 2 minutes. Through the feed tube, slowly add the oil to emulsify the mixture, until the dressing is silky smooth. Transfer to a bowl or squeeze bottle, cover, and refrigerate until needed.

2. Make the roulades: Put 1 chicken breast inside a large plastic zipper bag. With a cast-iron pan or other heavy pan, pound the breast evenly until flattened, as if for scaloppini. Remove from the bag and set aside. Repeat with the remaining chicken breasts.

3. In a medium bowl, crumble the cheese and beat in the sun-dried tomatoes and basil.

4. On a work surface, spread out a chicken breast and spread with one fourth of the cheese mixture. Roll up the breast as tightly as possible and tie in three places with kitchen string. Repeat with the remaining chicken breasts and cheese mixture.

5. Preheat the oven to 375°F. Season each chicken roll with salt and pepper and dredge lightly in flour, shaking off excess. In a heavy large ovenproof skillet or cast-iron pan, heat the oil over medium-high heat. Add the chicken rolls and cook, turning frequently, until golden brown on all sides, about 5 to 8 minutes total. Transfer the skillet to the oven and roast until the chicken is fully cooked (the breasts should register 165°F on an instant-read thermometer inserted into the thickest part), 8 to 10 minutes.

NOTES

- If you cannot find guava nectar, you can substitute 1 tablespoon guava paste, but you will also need to blend in ¼ cup water before adding the oil.

- You can eliminate the small risk of salmonella contamination in raw egg preparations by using pasteurized shell eggs.

6. Remove from the oven, transfer the rolls to a wire rack placed over a plate, and let cool for 30 minutes. Transfer to a container, cover, and refrigerate until cold, at least 2 hours and up to 1 day.

7. To serve, remove the strings, slice the rolls into ½-inch rounds, and divide them among serving plates. Roll up the slices of prosciutto and place them next to the chicken. Drizzle the roulade and prosciutto roll with the vinaigrette. Garnish with the tomatoes, frisée, olives, and thyme.

Ham Rolls with Celeriac and Apple

Ham's smoky, salty, sometimes spicy flavor profile takes to sweet flavors so well, especially apples and lingonberries. Celeriac (also known as celery root) provides a subtle celery flavor without the stringiness of celery.

Homemade mayonnaise is much more flavorful than store-bought, and can be enhanced with any number of flavorings. Pureed roasted garlic, curry powder, roasted red bell pepper, chipotle, and minced herbs are just a few possibilities.

1. In a medium bowl, combine the celeriac, apple, mayonnaise, and sour cream. Gently toss to combine. Season with salt and pepper.
2. To serve, spoon some celeriac salad on top of each slice of ham and roll up the ham into a tube or a coronet. Place a few lettuce leaves on the plate and drizzle with the oil. Spoon some lingonberry preserves at the front of the plate and sprinkle with the parsley. Garnish with the orange sections, bell pepper strips, and chives.

BASIC MAYONNAISE

Combine the egg yolks and mustard in a food processor. Blend until smooth. Season with salt, white pepper, and Worcestershire sauce. With the motor running, add the oil in a slow, steady stream through the feed tube, stopping once or twice to scrape down the sides. The mixture should become very thick. Add the lemon juice and blend until incorporated. Adjust the seasonings and transfer to a container. Cover and refrigerate until ready to use. (Fresh mayonnaise can be stored, covered, in the refrigerator for up to 4 days.) YIELD: 1³/4 CUP

> **NOTE** Trim away the outside of the celery root with a knife, as you would a pineapple, then chop or grate the white root for use in cooked or raw preparations. The celery-like stalks of the celeriac should be cut off from the root before storing. The hollow stalks are not cooked, except perhaps as a soup flavoring, though when fresh and not wilted they can be used as straws for Bloody Mary drinks.

YIELD: 10 SERVINGS

1 cup celeriac cut into thin strips (see Note)

¾ cup apple, peeled and cut into thin strips

3 tablespoons mayonnaise, store-bought or homemade (recipe follows)

3 tablespoons sour cream

Salt and freshly ground black pepper

10 thin slices smoked ham

Mixture of oak leaf and frisée lettuce

1 tablespoon olive oil

6 ounces lingonberry preserves (or huckleberry preserves or cranberry sauce)

1 tablespoon minced fresh flat-leaf parsley

1 navel orange, peel and pith removed, fruit cut into sections

1 medium red bell pepper, cored, seeded, and cut into thin strips

10 fresh chives

BASIC MAYONNAISE

2 large egg yolks (see Note, page 24)

1 teaspoon Dijon mustard

Salt

Freshly ground white pepper

Worcestershire sauce

1½ cups extra-virgin olive oil

1 tablespoon fresh lemon juice

Beef and Potato Empanadas with Chimichurri Sauce

YIELD: 30 SMALL EMPANADAS

DOUGH

3⅓ cups all-purpose flour

2¼ teaspoons salt

½ cup (1 stick) cold unsalted butter, cut into ½-inch cubes

¼ cup cold shortening, cut into pieces

1 large egg

⅔ cup ice water

1½ tablespoons distilled white vinegar

FILLING

6 tablespoons olive oil

1½ cups finely diced onion

½ cup thinly sliced scallions, white and light green parts only

2 teaspoons minced garlic

8 ounces lean ground beef

2 teaspoons ground cumin

2 teaspoons dried oregano

1 teaspoon salt

1 teaspoon freshly ground black pepper

½ pound potato, diced (about 2 cups)

¼ cup raisins, coarsely chopped, or diced red bell peppers

2 hard-cooked eggs, finely chopped

1 large egg, separated

¼ teaspoon paprika

¼ teaspoon sugar

Chimichurri Sauce (recipe follows)

E mpandas can be savory or sweet, baked or fried. If you cut larger pastry circles using the lid from a 32-ounce yogurt container as a template, they'll be the perfect size for a delicious lunch served with a salad.

1. Make the dough: In a large bowl, whisk together the flour and salt. Using your fingertips, a pastry blender, or two knives, work the butter and shortening into the flour until the mixture resembles coarse meal.

2. In a small bowl, beat together the egg, water, and vinegar with a fork. Using the fork, slowly stir the egg mixture into the flour mixture, just until incorporated. (Alternatively, combine the flour, salt, butter, and shortening in a food processor and pulse 4 times. Add the egg mixture and pulse 3 to 5 times, until it just comes together.)

3. Transfer the dough to a lightly floured surface and press the dough with the heel of your hand once or twice, folding it over in between, to bring it together. Pat the dough into a disk, cover it with plastic wrap, and refrigerate for at least 1 hour or up to 2 days.

4. Make the filling and assemble the empanadas: In a heavy skillet, heat 2 tablespoons of the oil over medium heat. Add the onion and scallions and cook, stirring, for 5 minutes. Add the garlic and cook, stirring, for 3 minutes. Transfer the contents of the pan to a bowl and set aside.

5. In the same skillet, heat 2 tablespoons of the oil over medium heat. Add the beef and cook, stirring gently to break up any lumps, until browned, about 5 minutes. Drain off any excess fat from the pan and return to the heat. Add the onion mixture to the beef, stirring well, then add the cumin, oregano, salt, and pepper. Cook, stirring, for another 2 minutes. Transfer the mixture to a bowl and let cool. Wipe out the pan.

6. In the same skillet, heat the remaining 2 tablespoons oil over high heat. Add the potato and cook, stirring, for 1 minute. Reduce the heat to low and cook, stirring, until tender, about 3 minutes more. Remove from the heat and let cool completely. When cool, add to the beef mixture, along with the raisins and chopped eggs. Gently mix just until incorporated. Let cool completely before filling the empanandas. (The filling can be stored, covered, in the refrigerator for up to 1 day.)

7. Preheat the oven to 375°F. Lightly butter two rimmed baking sheets or line them with parchment paper.

8. On a lightly floured surface, roll out the dough to a ⅛-inch thickness and cut rounds with a 3- to 3½-inch cutter. Working with one round at a time, place a heaping teaspoon of the beef filling in the center of the circle, leaving an ample border. Dip a small pastry brush into the egg white and brush along the entire edge of the circle of dough, lightly dampening it. Fold the empanada in half to enclose the filling, then press the edges together firmly. With the tines of a fork dipped in flour, crimp the edges of the empanada and place each on a prepared baking sheet. Repeat with the remaining dough and filling.

9. In a small bowl, beat the egg yolk with 1 teaspoon water, the paprika, and the sugar. Evenly brush all exposed parts of the sealed empanadas with the egg yolk mixture. Bake for 15 to 20 minutes, until golden brown. Serve warm or at room temperature with the chimichurri sauce for dipping.

CHIMICHURRI SAUCE

In the bowl of a blender or food processor, combine the oil, parsley, lime juice, vinegar, oregano, garlic, and crushed red pepper. Blend for about 10 seconds on medium speed, or until the sauce is blended. Season with cayenne pepper, salt, and black pepper.

CHIMICHURRI SAUCE

½ cup olive oil

¼ cup chopped fresh parsley

2 tablespoons fresh lime juice

1 tablespoon rice vinegar

2 teaspoons chopped fresh oregano, or 1 teaspoon dried oregano

1½ teaspoons finely minced garlic

¼ teaspoon crushed red pepper

Cayenne pepper

Salt and freshly ground black pepper

Grilled Prosciutto-Wrapped Figs
Stuffed with Gorgonzola and Walnuts

his flavorful combination of sweet, salty, and creamy will pair deliciously with sparkling wine or Champagne. Goat cheese makes a fine substitute for the Gorgonzola.

1. In a small saucepan, combine the vinegar, sugar, and red pepper flakes and bring to a simmer over medium heat. Cook until reduced to about ⅓ cup, about 5 minutes. Remove from the heat and let cool.

2. Soak the bamboo skewers (if using) in warm water for at least 30 minutes to prevent charring while cooking.

3. Brush the cut side of each fig with some of the vinegar mixture and fill with about 1 teaspoon of cheese. Press a walnut piece into the cheese, then wrap each fig half crosswise with a strip of prosciutto. Brush each wrapped fig half very lightly with oil.

4. Preheat a grill to medium-high. Thread 3 fig halves on each skewer and grill on all sides very carefully so that the fig is heated through and the prosciutto is slightly crisp, 5 to 6 minutes.

5. Meanwhile, in a medium bowl, whisk 1 teaspoon of the remaining vinegar mixture with 1 tablespoon oil. Season with salt and pepper. Add the arugula and toss until evenly coated. Divide the arugula among 4 plates.

6. Remove the figs from the skewers and arrange on the arugula. Drizzle each fig with a little of the remaining vinegar mixture. Top with Parmigiano-Reggiano and serve immediately.

YIELD: 4 SERVINGS

½ cup balsamic vinegar

¼ teaspoon sugar

⅛ teaspoon crushed red pepper

4 (8-inch) bamboo or metal skewers (see Note, page 34)

6 fresh Black Mission figs, ripe but not too soft, halved lengthwise, or 6 drained canned figs

4 ounces Gorgonzola cheese

12 large walnut pieces, toasted

12 (1-by-5-inch) thin strips of prosciutto (about 2 ounces)

2 to 3 tablespoons extra-virgin olive oil

Salt and freshly ground black pepper

2 cups baby arugula

Grated Parmigiano-Reggiano cheese

CHAPTER 2

SKEWERS, KEBABS, AND BROCHETTES

Skewers and kebabs are always a huge hit on board our ships. Whenever I put together a menu for a Holland America Line special event, I invariably include at least one of these appetizers for the cocktail hour. During the menu creation process, I think first in terms of creating an array of different visual sensations—and including a skewer or two is a fast way to add some real drama to the collection of appetizers that will get the party going.

I love the potential for architecture and intriguing artistic composition of ingredient elements that skewers offer. First, while so many finger foods need to be built up on a plate vertically, skewers give you the option of a single-serving appetizer composed horizontally. Thumb through the pages and see the stunning presentations, such as the Brochette of Vegetables with Quinoa Salad or the dramatic Chicken Teriyaki Skewers with Leeks and Sesame Spinach, and you'll begin to see what I mean.

Then, of course, there's the flavor profile. Start with anything—lamb, shrimp, vegetables, chicken, pork, scallops, you name it. Then add aromatic spice blends and marinades to imbue the ingredients with rich, complex flavors that stimulate the appetite even as they satisfy it. In fact, one of the things you need to consider when planning to use these as appetizers is to make sure your guests know that a full meal is coming—these skewers and kebabs are so addictive, it's easy to make a whole meal of them.

Speaking of easy, another factor that highly recommends these recipes is that the cooking time is super short. Make all the marinades and rubs in advance and let the flavor seep in, then, when it comes time for the party, a few minutes on the grill and these appetizers are sizzling hot and ready to go. Pair them with the flavor and texture foils of the recommended small salads and dip suggestions here, and you've presented your guests with a striking start to an unforgettable meal.

Grilled Lamb Kebabs with Tzatziki

YIELD: 4 TO 6 SERVINGS

½ teaspoon cumin seeds, toasted

2 large cloves garlic

2 teaspoons salt

1 teaspoon freshly ground black pepper

1 tablespoon chopped fresh cilantro, or 1½ teaspoons dried cilantro

½ teaspoon chopped fresh oregano, or ¼ teaspoon dried oregano

⅛ teaspoon cayenne pepper, or to taste

1 tablespoon fresh lemon juice

3 tablespoons extra-virgin olive oil

2 to 2½ pounds boneless leg of lamb, excess fat trimmed, meat cut into ½-inch cubes

12 (8- to 10-inch) metal or bamboo skewers (see Note)

Olives, slices red onion, parsley, and grape tomatoes, for garnish

TZATZIKI

1 large English hothouse (seedless) cucumber, peeled, halved lengthwise, and seeded

2 cups plain yogurt

1 to 2 tablespoons fresh lemon juice

2 medium cloves garlic, minced

2 tablespoons minced fresh parsley

1 tablespoon minced fresh dill

½ teaspoon freshly ground black pepper

Pinch of salt

2 tablespoons extra-virgin olive oil

Half-inch cubes of lamb are just the right size for an appetizer. Use 1-inch cubes (and increase the grilling time) if you want to serve this as a main dish.

1. Toast the cumin seeds in a small, dry heavy skillet over medium heat, shaking constantly, until fragrant, about 2 minutes. Transfer the cumin to a mortar and pestle and break up the seeds into smaller bits. Add the garlic, salt, and black pepper and mash the ingredients together until the garlic forms a paste. Mash in the cilantro, oregano, and cayenne. Transfer the mixture to a large bowl and whisk in the lemon juice and oil. Add the lamb and toss to coat. Cover and marinate in the refrigerator for at least 4 hours or overnight.

2. Soak the bamboo skewers (if using) in warm water for at least 30 minutes. Preheat a charcoal, gas, or electric grill to medium-hot (when you can hold your hand 5 inches above the rack for 3 to 4 seconds).

3. Thread the lamb cubes on the skewers, leaving a little space between pieces (for even cooking). Grill the kebabs on an oiled rack set 5 to 6 inches over the heat source; turn occasionally until grill marks appear on each side, 3 to 4 minutes total for medium-rare. (Alternatively, the kebabs can be broiled 3 to 4 inches from the heat element or grilled in several batches in a large well-seasoned ridged grill pan over medium-high heat.) Transfer the kebabs to plates and garnish with olives, red onions, parsley sprigs, and grape tomatoes. Serve with the tzatziki.

NOTE Use metal skewers if you have them; they will give the best results. However, good-quality, heavy bamboo skewers are attractive and come in many sizes. Some are even flat, have handles, or have double prongs. They can be reused and won't burn as easily as bamboo skewers that are available in grocery stores. Purchase heavy-duty bamboo skewers from Asian specialty markets or online, such as from Amazon.

TZATZIKI

1. Coarsely grate the cucumber; place in a strainer and let stand at room temperature until most of the liquid drains out, about 3 hours. Discard the liquid. Pat dry to remove excess moisture.

2. In a glass or ceramic bowl, combine the yogurt, lemon juice, garlic, parsley, dill, pepper, and salt. Stir until blended. Add the cucumber and stir to combine. Adjust the seasoning. Cover and refrigerate for at least 1 hour and preferably overnight, to allow the flavors to blend. Before serving, drizzle the top with the oil. YIELD: 3 CUPS

Pacific-Style Shrimp Brochettes with Asian Slaw

YIELD: 5 OR 10 SERVINGS

1½ tablespoons soy sauce

1 tablespoon finely minced jalapeño pepper

2 teaspoons bourbon

2 teaspoons fresh lime juice

2 teaspoons toasted sesame oil

2 teaspoons finely minced garlic

2 teaspoons tightly packed light brown sugar

¼ teaspoon ground cumin

1 pound large shrimp (21 to 25), peeled and deveined (see Notes)

10 (6- to 8-inch) metal or bamboo skewers (see Note, page 34)

½ red bell pepper, cut into ½-inch squares

½ red onion, cut into ½-inch squares

½ green bell pepper, cut into ½-inch squares

10 pieces Boston lettuce

Asian Slaw (recipe follows)

1 cup homemade Peanut Dipping Sauce, store-bought or homemade (recipe follows)

2 scallions, white part plus 2 inches green, very thinly sliced lengthwise

¼ cup chopped roasted peanuts

L ike many Asian-style skewers, these brochettes are delicious served with peanut dipping sauce. As an alternative, you can make double the amount of marinade and use half, warmed and slightly reduced, as a dipping sauce.

1. In a large glass or ceramic bowl, combine the soy sauce, jalapeño, bourbon, lime juice, sesame oil, garlic, brown sugar, and cumin. Add the shrimp and toss to coat. Cover and marinate in the refrigerator for 6 hours.

2. Soak the bamboo skewers (if using) in warm water for at least 30 minutes.

3. Remove the shrimp from the marinade and thread flat on the skewers (with the skewer going through the shrimp at head and tail), alternating with the vegetables in this order: shrimp, red bell pepper, onion, shrimp, green bell pepper, onion.

4. Preheat a charcoal, gas, or electric grill to medium-hot (when you can hold your hand 5 inches above the rack for 3 to 4 seconds). Grill the shrimp until just cooked through, 2 to 3 minutes on each side. (Alternatively, the brochettes can be broiled 3 to 4 inches from the heat element.)

5. To serve, divide the lettuce among serving plates and place 1 or 2 brochettes on each. Spoon some Asian slaw on each plate and drizzle with peanut sauce. Sprinkle with the scallions and chopped peanuts.

ASIAN SLAW

In a glass or ceramic bowl, toss the cabbage, carrot, scallions, onion, and sesame seeds until combined. In a small bowl, whisk the vinegar, soy sauce, and brown sugar until the sugar is dissolved. Drizzle the dressing on the cabbage mixture and toss to coat. Let stand for 30 minutes before serving. YIELD: 2 CUPS

PEANUT DIPPING SAUCE

In a food processor or blender, combine the peanut butter, soy sauce, brown sugar (if using), lime juice, ginger, and garlic. Process to combine. Season with *sambal oelek*. While the motor is running, drizzle in hot water to thin out the sauce—you may not need all of it. Pour the sauce into a serving bowl. Refrigerate until needed. (Bring the sauce to room temperature before serving.) YIELD: 1½ CUPS

ASIAN SLAW

2 cups finely shredded cabbage or coleslaw mix

½ cup grated carrot

2 medium scallions, white part plus 2 inches green, very thinly sliced lengthwise

3 tablespoons finely chopped onion

1 teaspoon sesame seeds

4 teaspoons rice vinegar

2 teaspoons soy sauce

2 teaspoons packed light brown sugar

PEANUT DIPPING SAUCE

¾ cup smooth peanut butter, preferably unsweetened

3 tablespoons low-sodium soy sauce

2 tablespoons light brown sugar (omit if peanut butter is sweetened)

Juice of 2 limes

2 teaspoons minced fresh ginger

1 clove garlic, minced

Sambal oelek (see Notes)

½ cup hot water

NOTES

- To peel and devein shrimp, pull the legs off the shrimp and peel away most of the shell, leaving only the tail shell intact. With a paring knife, devein the shrimp by cutting down the back of the shrimp and washing out the intestinal vein just below the surface.

- *Sambal oelek* is a Southeast Asian chile sauce that can be found in Chinese and Southeast Asian grocery stores.

Indonesian Pork Saté with Pickled Vegetables

This saté is served on board in the Tamarind restaurant as part of the Trail of Spices Saté Sampler. The slaw accompanying this saté is called *atjar* (the old spelling) in the Netherlands or *acar* by the Indonesians.

1. With a chef's knife, cut the pork into 3-inch-long strips that are 1½ inches wide and ¼ inch thick.
2. In a large glass or ceramic bowl, combine the two soy sauces, the lemon zest, garlic, ginger, and five-spice powder. Add the pork strips and toss to coat. Cover and marinate in the refrigerator for 2 hours.
3. Soak the bamboo skewers (if using) in warm water for at least 30 minutes.
4. Preheat a charcoal, gas, or electric grill to medium-hot (when you can hold your hand 5 inches above the rack for 3 to 4 seconds). Drain the marinade from the pork and thread the meat on the skewers, weaving in and out.
5. Grill the pork satés until just cooked through, 2 to 3 minutes on each side. (Alternatively, the satés can be broiled 3 to 4 inches from the heat element.)
6. To serve, divide the pickled vegetables and satés among the plates. Sprinkle with scallions and carrot and garnish with the cilantro sprigs. Serve with peanut dipping sauce.

PICKLED VEGETABLES (*ATJAR*)

In a large saucepan, combine 1 cup water, the vinegar, sugar, turmeric, coriander, and salt over medium-high heat. Bring to a boil and add the cabbage and carrots. Reduce the heat to low and simmer for 8 minutes. Remove from the heat, let cool to room temperature, cover, and refrigerate until ready to use.

YIELD: 6 SERVINGS

1½ pounds pork tenderloin

2½ tablespoons Indonesian sweet soy sauce (*ketjap manis*)

4 teaspoons Chinese or Japanese soy sauce

2 tablespoons finely grated lemon zest

1 tablespoon minced garlic

2 teaspoons ground ginger

1 teaspoon Chinese five-spice powder

30 (6-inch) metal or bamboo skewers (see Note, page 34)

2 scallions, white part plus 2 inches green, very thinly sliced lengthwise

1 small carrot, cut into thin strips

6 sprigs fresh cilantro

Peanut Dipping Sauce (pages 36–37)

PICKLED VEGETABLES (*ATJAR*)

1 cup white vinegar

5 tablespoons sugar

2 teaspoons turmeric

1 teaspoon ground coriander

¾ teaspoon salt

½ white cabbage, finely shredded

3 carrots, grated

Brochette of Vegetables with Quinoa Salad

YIELD: 6 SERVINGS

1 clove garlic, crushed

⅔ cup extra-virgin olive oil

2 tablespoons sherry vinegar

Salt and freshly ground black pepper

24 cherry tomatoes

24 white mushrooms, wiped clean and stemmed

4 large red bell peppers, cored, seeded, and cut into 1¼-inch squares

4 ears corn, shucked and cut into 6 rounds each

3 small onions, quartered

2 eggplants, cut into 1¼-inch cubes

12 (6- to 8-inch) metal or bamboo skewers (see Note, page 34)

Quinoa Salad (recipe follows)

QUINOA SALAD

1 cup quinoa

½ teaspoon salt

3 tablespoons seasoned rice vinegar

1 tablespoon walnut oil

½ cup walnuts, toasted and chopped (see Note)

⅓ cup dried cranberries

Salt and freshly ground black pepper

Quinoa is a high-protein grain from South America that's also a good source of iron and fiber. Toasting the grain prior to cooking adds a nutty flavor, but isn't necessary. Serve this salad at room temperature or slightly chilled.

1. Preheat a charcoal, gas, or electric grill to low. Soak the bamboo skewers (if using) in warm water for at least 30 minutes.
2. Meanwhile, drop the garlic into a cup with the oil and set aside to infuse for 30 minutes. Remove and discard the garlic.
3. In a small bowl, whisk the garlic-infused oil and the vinegar. Season with salt and pepper. Thread the vegetables through their centers onto the skewers, alternating them according to your own preference. Brush the vegetables generously with the oil mixture.
4. Grill the vegetables on an oiled rack set about 6 inches above the heat source, basting frequently with the seasoned oil, until the peppers are blistered and the tomato skins pop, 6 to 7 minutes on each side. Serve 2 skewers per person with some of the quinoa salad.

QUINOA SALAD

1. To remove the naturally occurring bitter saponins on the quinoa grains, place the quinoa in a sieve and rinse thoroughly under lukewarm running water, rubbing the grains together with your fingers. Drain thoroughly.
2. Heat a medium saucepan over medium-high heat. Add the quinoa to the pan and cook, stirring frequently, until toasted, about 5 minutes.
3. Add 1½ cups water and the salt to the quinoa and bring to a boil. Reduce the heat to low and cook, covered, until the water is absorbed and the quinoa is tender, about 15 minutes. Add a little more water, if necessary, and continue cooking if the water is absorbed but the quinoa still isn't tender. Remove from the heat and let cool in the pan, still covered.
4. Put the vinegar in a large glass or ceramic bowl and add the walnut oil in a thin stream, whisking constantly, until incorporated. Add the cooked quinoa, walnuts, and cranberries to the vinegar mixture and toss to combine. Season with salt and pepper. Serve at room temperature or slightly chilled. YIELD: 6 SERVINGS

NOTE To toast walnuts, preheat the oven to 350°F. Spread the walnuts on a baking sheet or in a shallow pan. Bake, stirring once or twice, until lightly browned and fragrant, 7 to 10 minutes. Let cool, then chop.

Chicken Brochettes with Tequila and Lime and Mango Banana Rum Sauce

S erve one large or two small brochettes per person, depending on whether you're offering them as "tapas" (to nibble with drinks) or as a regular appetizer that can be shared by two.

1. In a blender, combine the mango, banana, lime juice, tequila, brown sugar, salt, garlic, chile powder, and white pepper. Blend until smooth. Measure 1 cup of the mixture and transfer it to a glass or ceramic bowl and add the chicken. Toss to coat. Cover and marinate in the refrigerator for 4 hours.
2. Transfer the remaining mango mixture to a small saucepan and bring to a boil over medium-high heat. Reduce the heat to low and simmer, stirring, for 2 minutes. Strain through a fine sieve into a bowl. Stir in the rum. Cover and refrigerate the sauce until ready to serve.
3. Soak the bamboo skewers (if using) in warm water for at least 30 minutes.
4. Preheat a charcoal, gas, or electric grill to medium-hot (when you can hold your hand 5 inches above the rack for 3 to 4 seconds). Drain the marinade from the chicken and thread the chicken onto the skewers.
5. Grill the chicken brochettes, turning occasionally, until just cooked through, about 8 minutes. (Alternatively, the brochettes can be broiled 3 to 4 inches from the heat element.)
6. To serve, divide the brochettes among serving plates. Reheat the sauce just until warm and spoon some on each brochette (thin the sauce with a little water if necessary). Sprinkle with the pink peppercorns and pumpkin seeds and garnish with cilantro sprigs.

NOTE | To roast raw hulled pumpkin seeds, place about ¾ cup of seeds in a bowl and toss with 1½ teaspoons olive oil. Spread the seeds on a rimmed baking sheet and roast, stirring occasionally, in a preheated 300°F oven until they are golden brown, about 15 minutes.

YIELD: 6 SERVINGS

½ mango, peeled, pitted, and cut into chunks (about 3 ounces)

½ cup sliced banana

¼ cup fresh lime juice

¼ cup gold (oro) tequila

2 tablespoons tightly packed dark brown sugar

1½ teaspoons salt

1¼ teaspoons minced garlic

1 teaspoon ancho chile powder

½ teaspoon freshly ground white pepper

2 pounds skinless, boneless chicken breast halves, cut into 1-inch pieces

1 tablespoon rum

6 or 12 metal or bamboo skewers (see Note, page 34)

2 tablespoons whole pink peppercorns, crushed

¼ cup raw hulled pumpkin seeds, roasted (see Note)

Fresh cilantro sprigs

Chicken Teriyaki Skewers with Leeks and Sesame Spinach

YIELD: 10 SERVINGS

SESAME SPINACH

2½ pounds fresh spinach, rinsed and spun (or patted) dry

½ cup sesame seeds

½ cup chicken stock

2½ teaspoons sugar

5 teaspoons soy sauce

TERIYAKI CHICKEN SKEWERS

10 (8- to 10-inch) metal or bamboo skewers (see Note, page 34)

1 cup soy sauce

1 cup mirin

½ cup sake

½ cup sugar

3¾ pounds boneless, skinless chicken breast halves, cut into 1-inch pieces

1 pound leeks, white and pale green parts only, washed and cut crosswise into 1-inch sections, then cut lengthwise in half, keeping the layers intact

Y akitori negima is the most basic type of *yakitori*, and translates as "skewered teriyaki chicken with onion." Scallion pieces are used in Japan, but on board we like to use leeks. It's traditional to include both sake and mirin in the sauce. Sake is Japan's famous fermented rice wine. Mirin is a sweet rice wine that's lower in alcohol and is used for flavoring foods and in glazing sauces (a fine substitute for mirin is pale sweet sherry).

1. Make the sesame spinach: Bring a large pot of water to a boil and fill a large bowl three-quarters full with ice water. Plunge the spinach into the boiling water and cook, stirring, just until the leaves are wilted and bright green, about 30 seconds. With a strainer or skimmer, remove the spinach from the boiling water and transfer it to the bowl of ice water. Leave the blanched spinach in the ice bath until it's no longer warm, 2 to 3 minutes. Drain the spinach and gently squeeze it with your hands to remove excess water. With a chef's knife, chop the spinach into 1½-inch lengths. Set aside.

2. Meanwhile, in a heavy skillet, toast the sesame seeds over medium heat, shaking constantly, until fragrant and just golden, 2 to 3 minutes. Transfer the seeds to a large mortar and pestle, let cool, then crush. Transfer the sesame seeds to a glass or ceramic bowl and add the stock, sugar, and soy sauce. Stir until well mixed.

3. Right before serving, add the spinach to the dressing and gently mix (do not crush the spinach).

4. Make the teriyaki chicken skewers: Preheat a charcoal, gas, or electric grill or a broiler to medium-high heat. Soak the bamboo skewers (if using) in warm water for at least 30 minutes.

5. In a small saucepan, combine the soy sauce, mirin, sake, and sugar. Bring to a simmer over medium-low heat and cook until the sugar is dissolved and the sauce thickens slightly and is shiny, about 15 minutes. Pour one-quarter of the teriyaki sauce into a bowl and reserve for drizzling on the plates.

6. Thread the pieces of chicken and leek in alternating order on each skewer, leaving a 1-inch section free at the end to hold.

7. Grill the kebabs on an oiled rack set 5 to 6 inches over the heat source until the meat is three-quarters cooked, 1 to 2 minutes on each side. Brush each side generously with the teriyaki sauce from

the saucepan and grill on both sides until cooked through (about another 30 seconds on each side). (Alternatively, the *yakitori* can be broiled 3 to 4 inches from the heat element and basted frequently with the sauce.)

8. To serve, place some of the sesame spinach on each plate and lean a *yakitori* skewer on the spinach. Drizzle with the reserved teriyaki sauce and serve hot.

Lime-Marinated Grilled Scallops with Chipotle and Citrus Sauce

A little of the sauce goes a long way when served with these flavorful scallops, which feature a double dose of citrus.

1. Make the chipotle and citrus sauce: In a small saucepan, combine all the ingredients over medium heat. Cook, stirring, until heated through. Set aside. (The sauce can be stored, covered, in the refrigerator for up to 1 day. Rewarm before serving.)

2. Make the scallops: Preheat a charcoal, gas, or electric grill to medium-hot (when you can hold your hand 5 inches above the rack for 3 to 4 seconds).

3. In a glass or ceramic bowl, combine the oil, cilantro, lime juice, and lime zest. Add the scallops and toss to coat.

4. Thread the scallops onto the skewers and season with salt and pepper. Grill the scallops, turning occasionally, until just opaque in the center, about 3 minutes per side. (Alternatively, the brochettes can be broiled 3 to 4 inches from the heat element.)

5. To serve, arrange the scallops, on or off the skewers, on plates and drizzle the plates with the sauce. Garnish with the orange segments, zest, and cilantro sprigs.

YIELD: 4 SERVINGS

CHIPOTLE AND CITRUS SAUCE

¼ cup honey

2 tablespoons fresh orange juice

2 teaspoons finely grated lemon zest

1 teaspoon finely grated lime zest

¼ teaspoon minced chipotle in adobo sauce

SCALLOPS

2 tablespoons olive oil

2 tablespoons chopped fresh cilantro, plus a few sprigs for garnish

1½ tablespoons fresh lime juice

1 teaspoon finely grated lime zest

12 sea scallops, side muscle removed

4 (6- to 8-inch) metal or bamboo skewers (see Note, page 34)

Salt and freshly ground black pepper

1 navel orange, zested, pith removed, fruit cut into segments (zest set aside for garnish)

Chinese Beef Saté with Asian Broccoli Slaw

YIELD: 6 SERVINGS

(See photograph page 1)

ASIAN BROCCOLI SLAW

3 tablespoons rice vinegar

3 tablespoons soy sauce

1 tablespoon sugar

½ teaspoon dry mustard

2 tablespoons toasted sesame oil

½ cup peanut oil

2 cups purchased broccoli slaw (see Note)

1 cup grated carrots

6 scallions, thinly sliced

BEEF SATÉ

1½ pounds flank steak, skirt steak, or sirloin steak, at least ¾ inch thick

2 tablespoons light soy sauce

2 tablespoons hoisin sauce

2 tablespoons minced fresh garlic

1½ tablespoons minced fresh ginger

30 (8- to 10-inch) metal or bamboo skewers (see Note, page 34)

6 sprigs fresh cilantro

¼ cup chopped roasted peanuts

 his saté is served on board in the Tamarind restaurant as part of the Trail of Spices Saté Sampler. It recasts "beef and broccoli stir-fry" for the summertime grill. The dressing for the slaw makes more than you'll need. Refrigerated, it keeps for a month: Toss some with cut vegetables and cooked chicken for a flavorful light lunch.

1. Make the Asian broccoli slaw: In a small glass or ceramic bowl, whisk the vinegar, soy sauce, sugar, and dry mustard. Slowly whisk in the sesame oil and peanut oil.

2. Bring a pot of water to a boil and fill a medium bowl three quarters full with ice water. Plunge the broccoli slaw into the boiling water and cook, stirring, just until slightly wilted, about 30 seconds. With a strainer or skimmer, remove the broccoli slaw from the boiling water and transfer it to the bowl of ice water. Leave the blanched slaw in the ice bath until it's no longer warm, 2 to 3 minutes. Drain the slaw and pat dry with paper towels to remove excess water. Place the slaw in a large bowl.

3. Add the carrots and scallions to the blanched broccoli slaw. Rewhisk the dressing and measure out ¼ cup. Drizzle it on the vegetables, tossing to coat. Add more dressing if necessary. Cover the slaw and refrigerate until ready to use.

4. Make the beef satés: With a chef's knife, cut the beef against the grain into strips that are 1 inch wide and ¼ inch thick.

5. In a large glass or ceramic bowl, combine the soy sauce, hoisin sauce, garlic, and ginger. Add the beef strips and toss to coat. Cover and marinate in the refrigerator for at least 2 hours or overnight.

6. Soak the bamboo skewers (if using) in warm water for at least 30 minutes.

7. Preheat a charcoal, gas, or electric grill to medium-hot (when you can hold your hand 5 inches above the rack for 3 to 4 seconds). Drain the marinade from the beef and thread the meat onto the skewers, weaving in and out.

8. Grill the beef satés until just cooked through, 2 to 5 minutes on each side. (Alternatively, the satés can be broiled 3 inches from the heat element.) When it's done, the beef should be firm, not squishy, but not dried out, and should have a few crisp brown-black spots on each side.

9. To serve, divide the broccoli slaw among the plates and place 5 satés on each plate. Garnish with the cilantro sprigs and chopped peanuts.

NOTE | Broccoli slaw is raw broccoli stems grated and sold in bags in the refrigerator section of most grocery stores. If you cannot find it, simply trim, peel and coarsely grate fresh broccoli stems until you have 2 cups. Reserve the broccoli heads for another use.

CHAPTER 3

FRITTERS AND FRIED BITES

People love fried foods. And with good reason: If they're done correctly, they are absolutely delicious. But if when you think of fried foods you conjure heavy or greasy, the recipes in this chapter will likely change your assumptions.

When I think about frying as a cooking technique, the first thing that springs to my mind is seafood. Combining the inherent flakiness and lightness of a delicate fish with a flavorful batter crisped up quickly in hot oil creates a beautifully textured dish that surprises with its deep flavor and essential lightness.

In this chapter, you'll find highly requested fried appetizers featuring salt cod, fresh cod, shrimp, crabmeat, and calamari dressed up with flavors hailing from the Caribbean to the American Southwest and Asia to the South of France.

Another oft-requested appetizer on board cruises to all destinations are spring rolls. Here you'll find tangy barbecue chicken spring rolls in a classic East-meets-West interpretaion, as well as a favorite of many of our crewmembers, the Philippine pork spring roll. Don't miss the fried green tomato "sandwich," a sure-fire crowd-pleaser and always the first plate that comes back into the galley empty when being served as a passed appetizer at an onboard cocktail party.

In this chapter, you'll also find some of Holland America Line's signature flavored mayonnaises, including sun-dried tomato mayonnaise, spicy mayonnaise sauce, and Southwestern Aïoli (a garlicky mayonnaise). I like to make several of these to give my guests a whole range of flavors from which to choose. It's fun, and they love exploring the way each flavor profile completely changes the fritter or fried bite. Try it!

Fried Green Tomato "Sandwich" with Sun-Dried Tomato Mayonnaise

Thee "sandwiches" made with fried green tomatoes and a prosciutto and cheese filling can be short stack, or you can use three tomato slices each (with twice the filling).

1. Discard the ends of the tomatoes—you should get 3 good slices from each tomato. Season the tomato slices with salt and pepper. Put the flour in a shallow bowl. Pour the buttermilk into another shallow bowl. In a larger bowl, combine the cornmeal and panko, whisking until mixed.

2. One by one, dip both sides of each tomato slice into the flour, shaking off the excess, then into the buttermilk, then into the cornmeal mixture. Place each slice when coated on a baking sheet.

3. Preheat the oven to 200°F. Place a wire rack on a baking sheet and put it in the oven.

4. Pour ½ inch oil into a 10- or 12-inch frying pan or cast-iron skillet and heat the oil over medium-high heat. When a deep-frying thermometer registers 365°F and the oil is very hot but not smoking (a 1-inch cube of bread dropped into the oil should float to the surface almost immediately and brown within 1 minute), carefully slip 3 or 4 breaded tomato slices into the pan. Cook, turning them once, until they are golden brown, about 2 minutes per side. With a slotted spoon, transfer the tomato slices to the rack on the baking sheet in the oven to keep warm. Repeat with the remaining breaded tomatoes.

5. As the fried tomatoes accumulate in the oven, top some of the tomatoes with a slice of mozzarella and a slice of prosciutto. When all the tomatoes are fried, place the plain fried tomatoes on top of the ones with the cheese and prosciutto, to make many sandwiches. If necessary, return any sandwiches briefly to the oven to allow the mozzarella to melt slightly.

6. To serve, divide the fried tomato sandwiches among 6 serving plates. Top each with a dollop of sun-dried tomato mayonnaise and a small handful of arugula.

SUN-DRIED TOMATO MAYONNAISE

In a glass or ceramic bowl, whisk all the ingredients until well blended. Cover and refrigerate for at least 30 minutes before serving. (The mayonnaise will keep, covered, in the refrigerator for up to 2 days.)

YIELD: ABOUT ½ CUP

YIELD: 6 SERVINGS

6 hard green tomatoes, sliced ¼ inch thick

Salt and freshly ground black pepper

¾ cup all-purpose flour

¾ cup well-shaken buttermilk

1 cup yellow cornmeal

2 cups panko (Japanese bread crumbs)

Vegetable oil, for frying

6 to 12 (⅛-inch-thick) slices mozzarella or fontina cheese

6 to 12 slices prosciutto

2 cups baby arugula

SUN-DRIED TOMATO MAYONNAISE

½ cup mayonnaise, store-bought or homemade (page 27)

1 tablespoon minced moist sun-dried tomatoes from a jar

1 teaspoon sugar

1 teaspoon Italian seasoning

1 teaspoon fresh lemon juice

½ teaspoon minced garlic

Cod and Shrimp Fritters with Spicy Corn and Bell Pepper Dip

4 ounces cod fillet, skinned, poached, and chopped

4 ounces shrimp, raw or cooked, peeled and roughly chopped

1 cup all-purpose flour

1 large egg

2 tablespoons milk

1 tablespoon buttermilk

⅓ cup finely diced yellow onion

1 tablespoon minced garlic

1 teaspoon baking powder

½ teaspoon Worcestershire sauce

½ teaspoon Tabasco sauce

1 tablespoon minced fresh parsley

1 teaspoon fresh lemon juice

½ teaspoon Creole seasoning

Salt

Vegetable oil, for frying

1 ounce oak leaf lettuce leaves

1 ounce frisée lettuce

10 red endive leaves

10 fresh parsley sprigs

2 lemons, cut into wedges

Deep frying is a quick-cooking technique that heightens the texture and flavor of foods. For the best success, you need to understand some basic principles. First, foods fry best at temperatures between 350 to 375 degrees F, with larger items best at the lower range and smaller items best at the upper range. Second, every time you add food to hot oil, you lower the temperature slightly, so add foods slowly and never crowd a pan. Foods fried in oil that is at too low a temperature will be greasy and soggy.

1. In the bowl of a food processor, combine the cod, shrimp, flour, egg, milk, buttermilk, onion, garlic, baking powder, Worcestershire and Tabasco sauces, parsley, lemon juice, and Creole seasoning. Pulse until just blended but not completely smooth. Season with salt.

2. In a deep heavy skillet or saucepan, heat at least 1½ inches oil over medium-high heat until a deep-frying thermometer registers 350°F (at 350°F to 360°F a single kernel of popcorn dropped in the oil will pop). Line a wire rack with paper towels.

3. Using a 3-tablespoon scoop or another similar measure, drop mounds of fritter batter into the hot oil without crowding and fry until golden brown on all sides, 7 to 8 minutes. With tongs or a slotted spoon, transfer the fritters to the paper towels to drain. Repeat with the remaining fritter batter in several batches. Check the oil temperature between batches and adjust the heat accordingly.

4. To serve, line 10 shallow serving bowls with the lettuce leaves, placing them against the side to give the dish a little height. Arrange 2 or more fritters in each bowl. Garnish with the parsley sprigs and lemon wedges. Serve the dipping sauce alongside.

SPICY CORN AND BELL PEPPER DIP

In a glass or ceramic bowl, combine the mayonnaise, sour cream, corn, bell pepper, cilantro, chives, jalapeño, sugar, and maple syrup, folding with a spatula until mixed. Season with salt and pepper. Cover and refrigerate until ready to use. YIELD: 1¼ CUPS

¼ cup mayonnaise, store-bought or homemade (page 27)

¼ cup sour cream

¼ cup corn kernels, fresh or frozen (thawed), roughly chopped

3 tablespoons diced roasted red bell pepper, from a jar or home roasted (page 20)

2 tablespoons chopped fresh cilantro

1½ tablespoons minced fresh chives

1 tablespoon minced jalapeño pepper (or to taste)

2 teaspoons sugar

2 teaspoons maple syrup

Salt and freshly ground black pepper

Jamaican Salt Cod Fritters with Mango Relish and Spicy Mayonnaise

When making any kind of fritter or multiple-ingredient mixture that will be baked or fried, always sauté a small patty of the raw mixture in some oil or butter until fully cooked and then give it a taste. This allows you to check it for seasoning and add more salt, pepper, or spices as you like. The salt cod needs to be soaked well in advance, so plan ahead.

1. In a bowl, cover the salt cod with cold water and let soak for 18 to 24 hours, changing the water 4 or 5 times. Drain the salt cod, rinse it twice, and pick through it carefully to remove stray bone or skin pieces. Flake the cod into a large bowl.

2. Add the flour, baking powder, onions, bell peppers, scallions, jalapeño, curry powder, and thyme to the cod. Season with salt and black pepper. Stir to combine, adding just enough water (no more than ½ cup) to make a batter that coats the back of a spoon.

3. Pour ¾ inch oil into a 10- or 12-inch frying pan or cast-iron skillet and heat the oil over medium-high heat. Line a wire rack with paper towels.

4. When a deep-frying thermometer registers 375°F and the oil is very hot but not smoking (at 365°F a 1-inch cube of bread dropped into the oil should float to the surface almost immediately and brown within 1 minute), begin dropping tablespoonfuls of the cod mixture into the hot oil. Fry in batches until golden brown on all sides, about 1½ minutes. With a slotted spoon, transfer the fritters to the paper towels to drain. Check the oil temperature between batches and adjust the heat accordingly.

5. To serve, divide the fritters among serving plates and serve hot with the mango relish and spicy mayonnaise.

MANGO RELISH

In a small glass or ceramic bowl, combine the mango, bell pepper, scallions, cilantro, lime juice, and oil. Stir gently until well mixed. Season with the honey, salt, pepper, and ginger. Cover and refrigerate until needed. YIELD: 1½ CUPS

SPICY MAYONNAISE

In a small bowl, whisk the mayonnaise, cumin, and lime zest until blended. Season with the hot sauce. YIELD: ½ CUP

YIELD: 10 SERVINGS

8 ounces dried boneless salt cod

2 cups all-purpose flour

2 teaspoons baking powder

2 onions, finely diced

2 red bell peppers, finely diced

2 scallions, white and light green parts only, thinly sliced

1 jalapeño pepper, seeded and finely diced (or to taste)

1 teaspoon curry powder

½ teaspoon minced fresh thyme

Salt and freshly ground black pepper

Vegetable oil, for frying

MANGO RELISH

1 mango, peeled, seeded, and finely diced

½ red bell pepper, diced

2 scallions, white and light green parts only, thinly sliced

1 tablespoon chopped fresh cilantro

Juice of 1 lime

1 teaspoon extra-virgin olive oil

1 teaspoon honey

¼ teaspoon salt

Pinch of freshly ground black pepper

Pinch of ground ginger

SPICY MAYONNAISE

½ cup mayonnaise, store-brought or homemade (page 27)

1 teaspoon ground cumin

½ teaspoon finely grated lime zest

Hot sauce, preferably Jamaican

Corn and Crabmeat Fritters with Southwestern Aïoli

These fritters have pleasing texture and a touch of sweetness from the corn, which matches well with the smoky, citrus-flavored aïoli sauce.

1. In a large nonstick skillet, heat the butter over medium-high heat. Add the corn and onion and cook, stirring, until the onion is glossy and soft, 5 to 7 minutes. Transfer the corn mixture to a large bowl, cover, and refrigerate until slightly chilled.

2. In a medium bowl, whisk the flour, baking powder, salt, white pepper, and crushed red pepper; set aside. In a large bowl, whisk the milk and eggs until blended. Add the flour mixture very slowly, stirring with a rubber spatula until just combined. Very gently fold in the corn mixture and crabmeat.

3. In a deep heavy skillet or saucepan, heat the oil over medium-high heat until a deep-frying thermometer registers 350°F (at 350°F to 360°F, a single kernel of popcorn dropped in the oil will pop). Line a wire rack with paper towels.

4. Using a 3-tablespoon scoop or another similar measure, drop mounds of fritter batter into the hot oil without crowding and fry until golden brown on all sides, 7 to 8 minutes. With tongs or a slotted spoon, transfer the fritters to the paper towels to drain. Repeat with the remaining fritter batter in several batches. Check the oil temperature between batches and adjust the heat accordingly.

5. To serve, line 10 shallow serving bowls with the lettuces, placing them against the side to give the dish a little height. Arrange 2 or more fritters in each bowl. Garnish with the chives, lemon wedges, and tomato slices. Serve the Southwestern aïoli alongside.

SOUTHWESTERN AÏOLI

In a glass or ceramic bowl, whisk the mayonnaise, cilantro, garlic, lime juice, and chipotle. Season with salt and pepper. Cover and refrigerate until ready to use. YIELD: ABOUT 1 CUP

YIELD: 10 SERVINGS

2 tablespoons unsalted butter

2½ cups corn kernels, fresh or frozen (thawed)

½ cup finely chopped onion

2½ cups all-purpose flour

1 teaspoon baking powder

¼ teaspoon salt

¼ teaspoon freshly ground white pepper

Pinch of crushed red pepper

½ cup milk

2 large eggs

1½ pounds Dungeness crabmeat, picked over

3 cups vegetable oil, for frying

1 ounce oak leaf lettuce leaves

1 ounce frisée lettuce

1 plum tomato, cut into 8 to 10 slices

10 fresh chives

2 lemons, cut into wedges

Southwestern Aïoli (recipe follows)

SOUTHWESTERN AÏOLI

1 cup mayonnaise, store-bought or homemade (page 27)

2 tablespoons finely chopped fresh cilantro or chives

2 teaspoons minced garlic

Juice of 1 lime

1 teaspoon minced chipotle in adobo sauce or chipotle chile powder

Salt and freshly ground black pepper

Shrimp Tempura Indochine

YIELD: 10 SERVINGS

1½ cups cake flour (not self-rising), plus extra for dusting

½ cup rice flour (available at natural foods stores)

1½ teaspoons baking powder

1¼ pounds jumbo shrimp (2 per serving)

Salt and freshly ground black pepper

Vegetable oil, for frying

2½ cups sparkling water, chilled until very cold, or ice-cold water

Thai Green Papaya Salad (see page 104)

Garlic Chile Sauce (recipe follows)

20 fresh chives

GARLIC CHILE SAUCE

1 tablespoon vegetable oil

½ head garlic, peeled and finely minced

2 tablespoons finely minced onion

6 tablespoons Sriracha or other Asian hot chile sauce (such as Thai chile sauce)

2 tablespoons sugar

¼ cup ketchup

3 tablespoons chicken stock

1 tablespoon cornstarch mixed with 1 tablespoon water (if needed)

2 tablespoons seeded and minced Thai chiles or serrano chiles

Successful tempura is very light, and requires very cold batter, because cold batter will puff up as soon as it hits hot oil. You can keep the batter cold by nestling it in an ice bath, storing it in the freezer while you heat the oil, or even adding ice cubes to it if it starts to warm.

This recipe, from our onboard pan-Asian restaurant, Tamarind, brings together two beloved Japanese and Thai specialties: tempura and green papaya salad.

1. In a large bowl, whisk the flours and baking powder. Place the bowl in the freezer. Line a wire rack with paper towels.
2. Flatten each shrimp (to prevent curling during cooking) by making several shallow cuts across the inside curve of each shrimp, then pressing the shrimp on the cutting board. Season with salt and pepper and lightly dust with flour (which will help the batter adhere).
3. In a large heavy saucepan over medium-high heat, heat 3 inches oil over medium-high heat until a deep-frying thermometer registers 365°F and the oil is very hot but not smoking (a 1-inch cube of bread dropped into the oil should float to the surface almost immediately and brown within 1 minute).
4. While waiting for the oil to heat, very gradually whisk the cold sparkling water into the cold flour mixture, mixing only until the dry ingredients are moistened (overworking the batter, even simply to remove lumps, risks the batter becoming heavy).
5. With tongs or chopsticks, dip the shrimp, in batches, into the batter, and let the excess drip off. Fry a few shrimp at a time until golden, 2 to 3 minutes. With tongs, transfer the tempura to the paper towels to drain. Check the oil temperature between batches and adjust the heat accordingly.
6. Divide the tempura among serving plates. Place the green papaya salad and garlic chile sauce alongside and garnish with the chives.

GARLIC CHILE SAUCE

1. In a nonstick skillet, heat the oil over medium-high heat. Add the garlic and onion and cook, stirring, for 3 minutes. Add the Sriracha sauce and sugar and cook, stirring, for 2 minutes, until the mixture lightly caramelizes. Add the ketchup and stock and bring to a simmer.
2. Check for thickness: If the sauce is thin, stir in a bit of the cornstarch mixture. Stir in the fresh chiles and remove from the heat. Set aside until ready to serve. YIELD: 1¼ CUPS

Fried Calamari with Spicy Anchovy Mayonnaise

raham cracker crumbs make an unusual breading for calamari, but it's important to cook them immediately after breading to keep the crumbs from becoming soggy.

1. Cut the squid bodies into ¼-inch-thick rings. If the tentacles are large, halve or quarter them lengthwise.
2. In a deep heavy saucepan, heat the oil over medium-high heat until a deep-frying thermometer registers 375°F and the oil is very hot but not smoking (at 365°F a 1-inch cube of bread dropped into the oil should float to the surface almost immediately and brown within 1 minute). Line a wire rack with paper towels.
3. In a small bowl, combine the flour, graham cracker crumbs, and cardamom. In another bowl, lightly beat the eggs.
4. Working with one batch at a time, dip the squid in the eggs, shaking off any excess, then dredge it in the graham cracker mixture. Toss the calamari in a mesh strainer to shake off any excess coating. Immediately fry the batch of squid until golden brown, about 2 minutes. With tongs or a slotted spoon, transfer the calamari to the paper towels to drain. Season with salt. Repeat the breading and frying process for each additional batch. Check the oil temperature between batches and adjust the heat accordingly. Serve immediately with the spicy anchovy mayonnaise, lemon wedges, and, if desired, a garnish of endive leaves.

SPICY ANCHOVY MAYONNAISE

In a food processor, puree all the ingredients until smooth. Divide among 4 individual ramekins. Cover and refrigerate until ready to serve. YIELD: ABOUT ½ CUP

YIELD: 4 SERVINGS

8 ounces fresh or frozen small squid, cleaned (ink sac, cartilage, heads, and dark skin removed)

1½ quarts peanut or light olive oil, for frying

½ cup all-purpose flour

⅓ cup graham cracker crumbs

Pinch of ground cardamom

2 large eggs

Salt

4 lemon wedges

1 head Belgian endive, leaves separated (optional)

SPICY ANCHOVY MAYONNAISE

½ cup mayonnaise, store-bought or homemade (page 27)

6 to 8 anchovy fillets

2 tablespoons chopped fresh parsley

1 teaspoon fresh lemon juice

½ teaspoon cayenne pepper

Philippine Pork Spring Rolls with Spicy Asian Slaw

(See photograph page 6)

**YIELD: 50 BITE-SIZE
SPRING ROLLS**

25 *lumpia* wrappers, or "super-thin"-type Chinese spring roll wrappers, thawed if frozen

1 tablespoon all-purpose flour

4 teaspoons cold water

2 tablespoons vegetable oil

2 pounds ground pork

½ cup chopped scallions, white and light green parts only

4 cloves garlic, peeled and minced

2-inch piece of ginger, peeled and minced

1 cup grated carrots

½ cup finely diced jícama (optional)

1 dried red chile, finely chopped, or a generous pinch of crushed red pepper

¼ cup chopped fresh cilantro

1 to 2 tablespoons soy sauce

Freshly ground black pepper

Peanut or corn oil, for frying

olland America Line has many Filipino staff, and these spring rolls (called *lumpia*) are a taste of home for them. Feel free to substitute some chopped shrimp for 10 to 12 ounces of the pork— *lumpia* have numerous variations. The spicy Asian slaw and garlicky sweet dipping sauce are flavorful accompaniments.

1. With a serrated knife, cut the square *lumpia* wrappers in half diagonally so you have two stacks of triangular wrappers. Cover the *lumpia* wrappers loosely with a dampened cloth to keep them from drying out. In a small bowl, combine the flour with the cold water; set aside.

2. In a large nonstick skillet, heat the vegetable oil over medium-high heat. Add the pork, scallions, garlic, and ginger. Cook, stirring, until the pork is no longer pink, 10 minutes. Add the carrot, jícama (if using), and the dried chile. Cook, stirring, for 2 to 3 minutes. Pour off any excess oil and transfer the pork mixture to a large bowl. Stir in the cilantro and soy sauce. Cover and refrigerate until slightly chilled.

3. Place 1 wrapper on a work surface with the longest edge facing you (keep the remaining wrappers covered). Place a tablespoon of filling on the wrapper about ½ inch from the edge closest to you. Fold the two side corners toward each other and over the filling. Grasp the bottom edge of the wrapper and roll it up into a roll, stopping when 1½ inches of wrapper remain. Brush some of the flour mixture onto the last bit of wrapper (the flour will seal it) and finally finish rolling. Rest each finished *lumpia* on its seam while rolling the remainder. (To freeze and fry later, dip the seam side of the rolls briefly in very hot oil to seal them, then freeze the rolls for 30 minutes on a baking sheet. Transfer the rolls to freezer bags and store in the freezer for up to 3 months; do not thaw before frying.)

4. In a 12-inch cast-iron skillet or wok, heat at least 2 inches of oil over medium-high heat until a deep-frying thermometer registers 370°F and the oil is very hot but not smoking (at 365°F a 1-inch cube of bread dropped into the oil should float to the surface almost immediately and brown within 1 minute). Line a wire rack with paper towels.

5. Carefully add 3 or 4 *lumpia* to the hot oil and fry until golden brown, turning once and keeping them apart so they don't stick together, about 2 minutes (1 to 2 minutes longer if frying from frozen). Don't put too many *lumpia* in at once or the oil temperature will lower or the rolls will stick together. With tongs or a slotted spoon, transfer the rolls to the paper towels to drain. Repeat with the remaining *lumpia* in as many batches as necessary. Check the oil temperature between batches and adjust the heat accordingly.

6. To serve, divide the hot *lumpia* among serving plates. Spoon some of the spicy Asian slaw alongside, and serve each person a ramekin of sweet-and-sour chile sauce.

SPICY ASIAN SLAW

1. In a small saucepan over medium heat, combine the sugar and vinegar and stir until the sugar dissolves. Remove from the heat and add the jalapeño and ginger.

2. In a medium glass or ceramic bowl, combine the cabbage, bell pepper, and scallions. Pour the vinegar mixture over the cabbage mixture and toss to coat. Season with salt and pepper. (The slaw will keep, covered, in the refrigerator for up to 1 day.) Right before serving, sprinkle the slaw with the cilantro. YIELD: 5 CUPS

SWEET AND SOUR CHILE SAUCE

In a medium saucepan, combine the vinegar and ¾ water and bring to a boil over high heat. Stir in the sugar, garlic, ginger, chile, and ketchup; reduce the heat to low and simmer for 5 minutes. Stir in the cornstarch mixture and cook, stirring, until thickened slightly. Remove the pan from the heat and let cool. Transfer the sauce to a glass or ceramic bowl, cover, and refrigerate until needed. YIELD: 2 CUPS

SPICY ASIAN SLAW

3 tablespoons sugar

3 tablespoons seasoned rice vinegar

1 jalapeño pepper, seeded and thinly sliced into rings

2 teaspoons minced peeled fresh ginger

5 cups thinly sliced Napa cabbage

1 small red bell pepper, cut into thin strips

½ cup chopped scallions

Salt and freshly ground black pepper

¼ cup chopped fresh cilantro

SWEET AND SOUR CHILE SAUCE

1 cup unseasoned rice vinegar

1 cup sugar

2 teaspoons minced fresh garlic

1 teaspoon minced fresh ginger

1 teaspoon minced serrano chile or jalapeño pepper

2 teaspoons ketchup

2 teaspoons cornstarch mixed with 1 tablespoon water

NOTE | Philippine pork spring rolls are terrific for dipping, but not double-dipping, because their loose contents will fall out into the sauce when the roll is turned upside down. Serve the dipping sauce for these *lumpia* in ramekins and with a spoon, so guests can spoon the sauce into the *lumpia* after they've taken their first bite.

CHAPTER 4

TARTARES, CARPACCIOS, AND CEVICHES

If sophistication is on the menu for your next party, find your inspiration right here. This chapter is a collection of recipes that demonstrate the luxury of super-premium, fresh ingredients—served either raw or nearly raw.

Every great culinary tradition has its share of lightly seared or raw dishes. Ceviche, typically fresh fish marinated in citrus and spice, hails from South and Central America. Carpaccio, paper-thin slices of raw beef, veal, salmon or tuna dressed with a sauce, has its origins in Italy. Tartare, finely chopped raw meat or fish, is a classic French restaurant dish.

Thanks to the creativity of Holland America Line's culinary artists, you can enjoy sensational variations of these dishes that transcend even the brilliance of the originals.

For example, here you'll find Pineapple Carpaccio—my tropical twist on what's traditionally thought of as a meat or fish preparation; it looks like a work of art on the plate. Classic Steak Tartare becomes an exotic statement of indulgent luxury when paired with caviar and quail eggs. And a simple scallop ceviche becomes a stunningly refreshing appetizer, elegantly beautiful for hot weather when paired with watermelon, tomato, and mint.

Of course, all great cooking begins with the best-quality ingredients you can get your hands on, and when the recipe calls for little or no cooking, the superiority of the ingredients is even more crucial. At Holland America Line, we pride ourselves on our ability to source the finest, freshest ingredients available in the world. Treat your guests to the same: Serve one or more of these spectacular special appetizers, and they will feel as spoiled and pampered as they would at the VIP table on board one of our liners.

Pineapple Carpaccio with Strawberries, Goat Cheese Whipped Cream, Pink Pepper, and Fig Balsamic Vinegar

GOAT CHEESE WHIPPED CREAM

½ cup heavy cream

2 tablespoons goat cheese, at room temperature

PINEAPPLE CARPACCIO

1 whole pineapple, peeled

12 whole strawberries, hulled and sliced

¼ cup fig balsamic vinegar

2 teaspoons whole pink peppercorns

Fresh mint or basil sprigs

The word *carpaccio* is generally used to describe thin slices of raw beef served as an appetizer. It apparently originated at Harry's Bar in Venice in the 1950s and is named for Venetian painter Vittore Carpaccio. Over time, very thin slices of raw fish and fruit have also come to be called carpaccio. Whatever the type you wish to make, creating carpaccio is easier with a mandoline slicer (see Note below). In this appetizer, contrasting flavors and textures complement each other in an intriguing and delicious way.

1. Make the goat cheese whipped cream: With a whisk or electric beaters, whip the cream until fluffy. Soften the goat cheese with the back of a spoon, then whisk it into the cream until incorporated. Set aside in the refrigerator.

2. Make the pineapple carpaccio: With a mandoline slicer or a serrated knife, cut the pineapple crosswise into very thin round slices. Overlap 6 to 8 slices in the center of each serving plate. Reserve any remaining pineapple for another use.

3. Arrange sliced strawberries in the center of each pineapple pile and top with a spoonful of goat cheese whipped cream. Drizzle 1 to 2 teaspoons fig balsamic vinegar decoratively onto the pineapple and garnish with the pink peppercorns. Place a mint or basil sprig into the whipped cream and serve immediately.

NOTE | A mandoline is a useful tool for cutting very thin slices of fruits and vegetables. Mandolines usually come with various adjustable blades and range in price and quality, depending on the materials with which they're made (generally metal or plastic). Most have built-in safety features to protect fingers and hands from their razor-sharp blades, but wearing cut-resistant gloves while operating a mandoline can provide additional security.

Steak Tartare with Sliced Eggs

The most important part of steak tartare is very fresh, good-quality beef. The remaining ingredients are a cinch to come by. That said, applying a crowning touch of a halved, hard-cooked quail egg topped with a little caviar will lift this dish to the heavens.

1. With a sharp knife, finely chop the beef and put it in a large bowl. Add the onion, gherkins, chopped parsley, anchovies, capers, and egg yolk and stir until well combined. Season with the Tabasco and Worcestershire sauces, paprika, brandy, salt, and pepper. Cover and chill in the refrigerator for at least 30 minutes, until ready to serve.

2. Mold the chilled steak mixture into one patty per plate. Top with an egg slice (or half a quail egg topped with caviar). Garnish with onions, gherkins, chopped parsley, anchovies, capers, egg white, egg yolk, and parsley sprig. Serve immediately with the toast strips.

YIELD: 4 SERVINGS

1 pound beef tenderloin, trimmed of all fat and sinew

3 tablespoons minced red onion, plus extra for garnish

2 tablespoons minced sour gherkins, plus extra for garnish

1 tablespoon minced fresh parsley, plus extra for garnish

6 anchovy fillets, minced, plus extra for garnish

1 tablespoon capers, rinsed, drained, and chopped, plus extra for garnish

1 large egg yolk (see Note, page 24)

Tabasco sauce

Worcestershire sauce

Pinch of paprika

Dash of brandy

Salt and freshly ground black pepper

2 large eggs, hard cooked (or 4 quail eggs), 1 peeled and sliced and 1 with white and yolk chopped separately

2 tablespoons black or Russian caviar (optional)

Fresh parsley sprigs

4 slices white bread, toasted and cut into strips

Tuna Tartare with Shrimp

1¼ pounds sushi-quality tuna

2 tablespoons minced scallion, white and light green parts only

1 tablespoon chopped fresh cilantro

1 tablespoon fresh lime juice

2½ teaspoons soy sauce

2½ teaspoons fresh orange juice

2 teaspoons minced fresh garlic

1 teaspoon minced fresh ginger

¾ teaspoon minced jalapeño pepper

¼ teaspoon ground cumin

Salt and freshly ground black pepper

3 limes, cut into wedges

2 naval oranges, peels blanched, flesh cut into segments (see Note)

10 cherry tomatoes, quartered

1 tablespoon sesame oil or extra-virgin olive oil

10 extra-large shrimp, cooked and peeled

Cocktail sauce, store-bought or homemade (recipe follows)

Fresh parsley sprigs

COCKTAIL SAUCE

½ cup ketchup

¼ cup chili sauce

2 tablespoons horseradish, preferably freshly grated

2 tablespoons fresh lemon juice

2 teaspoons minced scallion, green parts only

½ teaspoon Worcestershire sauce

Tabasco sauce

Soy sauce is a deep and delicious seasoning for raw tuna, but too much soy can overpower tuna's delicate flavor and muddy its lovely color. If you taste the tartare and think it needs more seasoning, resist the urge to add more soy and just use salt instead.

1. With a sharp knife, dice the tuna into ¼-inch cubes and put it in a stainless-steel bowl sitting in a larger bowl of ice. Add the scallion, cilantro, lime juice, soy sauce, orange juice, garlic, ginger, jalapeño, and cumin. With a rubber spatula, gently fold the mixture until combined. Season with salt and black pepper. Cover the bowl and refrigerate until the mixture is cold, 3 to 4 hours.

2. To serve, attractively arrange the lime wedges, orange segments, and tomatoes on each serving plate. Brush the inside of a 2- to 3-inch ring mold with some of the sesame oil and position it in the center of a plate. Fill it with some of the tuna mixture, patting down somewhat firmly, and carefully remove the mold. Repeat with the remaining tuna on the remaining plates. Surround each tuna mound with a shrimp and some blanched orange peel. Spoon some cocktail sauce onto each plate and garnish with a parsley sprig. Serve immediately.

COCKTAIL SAUCE

In a small glass or ceramic bowl, whisk the ketchup, chili sauce, horseradish, lemon juice, scallions, and Worcestershire sauce. Season with Tabasco sauce. Cover and refrigerate until ready to use.

YIELD: ABOUT 1 CUP

NOTE | To make the two kinds of orange garnish for this recipe, start by slicing the ends off the two oranges. To blanch the peel, use a peeler or paring knife to remove the orange part (but not the bitter pith) of each orange. Cut the peel into thin strips and drop into boiling water for 3 minutes. Drain, rinse the peels, and repeat the boiling process a second time in fresh water. To cut the orange into segments, use a paring knife to completely remove the pith on the two trimmed oranges, then cut out the sections between the membranes. You can measure 2½ teaspoons juice collected while segmenting for the tartare.

Pesto-Stuffed Beef Carpaccio with Truffle Dressing

YIELD: 4 SERVINGS

DRESSING

3 tablespoons walnut oil

2 tablespoons balsamic vinegar

2 tablespoons port

1 tablespoon truffle juice (see Note)

2 tablespoons minced shallot

Salt and freshly ground black pepper

Sugar

CARPACCIO

1¼ pounds beef tenderloin, trimmed of all fat and sinew

1 cup spinach leaves

1 cup fresh basil leaves

2 cloves garlic, smashed

½ cup blanched almonds, chopped

½ cup extra-virgin olive oil

Salt and freshly ground black pepper

4 radicchio leaves or red endive leaves

4 green endive leaves

8 frisée lettuce leaves

4 baby red oak lettuce leaves

2 cherry tomatoes, halved

4 fresh chives

This colorful, beautiful, and very flavorful appetizer is perfect for a special occasion.

1. Make the dressing: In a blender, combine the oil, vinegar, port, and truffle juice. Blend until thoroughly mixed. Transfer to a small glass or ceramic bowl. Whisk in the shallot. Season with salt, pepper, and sugar. Set aside.

2. Make the carpaccio: Cut the beef tenderloin open lengthwise without cutting it completely through. Place it flat on a sheet of plastic wrap and cover it with another sheet of plastic. With a rolling pin, pound the tenderloin until it's evenly flattened to ¼ inch thick. Cover with plastic wrap and refrigerate until needed.

3. In a blender, combine the spinach, basil, garlic, almonds, and olive oil. Blend until smooth. Season with salt and pepper.

4. Remove the plastic wrap from the beef tenderloin. Spread the spinach mixture over one side of the beef and roll it up like a cinnamon roll. Place the tenderloin roll on a sheet of aluminum foil and wrap it up tightly, sealing the ends. Chill it in the freezer for 4 to 5 hours.

5. Remove the beef from the freezer and unwrap it. With a sharp knife, slice it, still frozen, into very thin rounds. Arrange 6 to 8 slices in an attractive design on each of 4 serving plates.

6. To serve, arrange a lettuce bouquet in the center of the carpaccio. Garnish with a tomato half. Drizzle the carpaccio with some of the dressing. Garnish with a chive and serve immediately.

NOTE Canned (or jarred) truffles come packed with a small amount of liquid, which is actually a by-product of the pressure-cooking process. That liquid is fine for this recipe, as would be truffle juice that is sold on its own (without the truffles), which is generally more expensive. Instead of truffle juice, feel free to substitute 1 tablespoon of truffle oil for 1 tablespoon of the walnut oil.

Scallop Ceviche with Watermelon, Tomatoes, and Mint

his light and refreshing ceviche uses the firmer, crunchier light pink portion of the watermelon for texture, and the juice of the sweeter, red portion for flavor.

1. Lay the scallops out in a shallow ceramic dish. Douse them with the lemon and lime juices and vinegar. Sprinkle with the salt, shallot, and garlic and allow to marinate for at least 30 minutes and up to 2 hours. Drain the scallops (discard the marinade) and chill in the refrigerator.

2. Cut the watermelon into slices and then cut away the sweet dark-pink portion; set aside. Cut a strip (an inch or so thick) of the light-pink portion that sits about ¼ inch above the green rind (discard the rind). Chop the light-pink watermelon into ¼-inch dice and measure 1 cup; put in a bowl and set aside (cover and chill if not using immediately). Grate the sweet dark-pink watermelon pieces into a sieve (or process in a food processor and strain) to obtain ¾ cup watermelon juice; put the juice in a separate bowl (cover and chill).

3. To serve, arrange the scallop disks in the center of 4 shallow serving bowls or martini glasses. Spoon some of the watermelon juice over them and drizzle with some oil. Toss the light-pink watermelon with the tomatoes and spoon the mixture into the center and around the scallops. Scatter the mint over each bowl, add a lime wedge, and serve chilled.

YIELD: 4 SERVINGS

4 large sea scallops, side muscle removed, sliced into disks

2 tablespoons fresh lemon juice

2 tablespoons fresh lime juice

2 tablespoons rice vinegar

1 tablespoon Maldon sea salt

1 tablespoon chopped shallot

½ tablespoon minced garlic

8 ounces watermelon (to produce 1 cup diced light-pink portion and ¾ cup watermelon juice)

4 teaspoons olive oil

½ cup grape or cherry tomatoes, quartered

10 fresh mint leaves, torn

Lime wedges

Salmon Ceviche with Orange Zest and Capers

1 tablespoon canola oil

8 ounces skinless salmon fillet, preferably wild

2 teaspoons fresh lime juice

Salt and freshly ground black pepper

⅓ cup finely diced papaya, plus extra for garnish

¼ cup cored, seeded, and finely diced tomato

3 tablespoons finely diced red onion

1 teaspoon finely grated orange zest

2 tablespoons capers, roughly chopped

1½ tablespoons roughly chopped cilantro, plus extra for garnish

1 tablespoon minced roasted jalapeño pepper (see page 20)

1½ tablespoons extra-virgin olive oil

1½ cups finely shredded iceberg lettuce

2 limes, cut into wedges

20 very thin slices French bread, toasted

he salmon for this ceviche is lightly seared but not fully cooked, to add taste and textural contrasts.

1. In a heavy skillet, heat the canola oil over medium-high heat. Add the salmon to the pan and cook for about 30 seconds on each side, until seared (do not fully cook). Gently remove the salmon, place on a plate, and let cool to room temperature. Cover the salmon with plastic wrap and refrigerate for 1 to 2 hours, or until completely chilled.

2. With a chef's knife, dice the salmon into ¼-inch pieces. Put in a stainless-steel bowl and gently toss with the lime juice. Season with salt and pepper and let marinate for 5 minutes.

3. Add the papaya, tomato, onion, orange zest, capers, cilantro, jalapeño, and olive oil. With a rubber spatula, gently fold until combined. Adjust the seasonings. Cover with plastic wrap and refrigerate for up to 4 hours.

4. To serve, divide the iceberg lettuce among 10 martini glasses and top with the ceviche. Garnish with papaya and cilantro and serve with the lime wedges and toasted bread slices.

CHAPTER 5

SMALL BITES

While many of the culinary events you will attend aboard a Holland America Line ship are formal pull-out-all-the-stops affairs that start with a fabulous Champagne and move up the luxury scale from there, sometimes an onboard gathering will be far more casual in nature—but just as delicious. Likewise, not every gathering you have at your home will call for an epic culinary adventure. Still, if you're going to the trouble to entertain, you'll want to put your best foot forward even for a casual get-together.

In this chapter, you'll find everything you need to put out a great spread of casual appetizers that people will absolutely love. In fact, I wouldn't be surprised if you adopted several of these as "staples" in your entertaining repertoire. Each is as fun to eat as it is tasty and truly fits the bill for light nibbling, whether it be for a gathering to watch a football game, a book-club party, or as a prelude to a lovely old-fashioned home-cooked meal like a roast.

This is not to say, however, that any one of these wouldn't be right at home for a more formal event. Even the sliders are a class act for a special occasion. In fact, one of the things I truly love about this collection of small bites is that the recipes are highly versatile: Make the Greek Meatballs for an elegant holiday meal starter, or bring them to a potluck dinner. Ideal for easy entertaining, the Sweet Onion Tartlets and Tomato and Goat Cheese Tartlets can be mostly prepared a day ahead of time, and then you can finish them up right before your guests arrive, filling your home with a wonderful savory aroma.

In fact, these recipes make for such wonderful, flavorful eating, I guarantee you'll find yourself making batches of one or more of these when no one is coming over at all, and you just want something great to eat while you settle in to watch your favorite TV show. I know I do!

Greek Meatballs

or a cocktail party, spear each meatball on a short skewer next to a cherry tomato with a mint leaf in between. Or tuck a meatball into a pita pocket triangle.

1. In a small skillet, heat the oil over medium heat. Add the scallions and garlic and cook, stirring, until softened, about 1½ minutes. Transfer the mixture to a bowl and sprinkle with the salt, cinnamon, cumin, and allspice. Add the lamb, bread crumbs, and egg, working everything together thoroughly with your hands. Cover with plastic wrap and refrigerate for at least 30 minutes and up to 1 day.

2. Line a baking sheet with plastic wrap and prepare a medium bowl of cold water. Form 1-inch meatballs, dipping your hands into the cold water to keep the meat from sticking to them. Arrange them on the prepared baking sheet.

3. Pour at least ½ inch of oil into a 10- or 12-inch frying pan or cast-iron skillet and heat until a deep-frying thermometer registers 350°F (at 350°F to 360°F a single kernel of popcorn dropped into the oil will pop). Line a wire rack with paper towels.

4. Add a batch of meatballs carefully to the hot oil without crowding. Fry on one side for 2 minutes, then on the other side until golden brown. With a slotted spoon, transfer the meatballs to the paper towels to drain. Repeat with another batch of meatballs. Check the oil temperature between batches and adjust the heat accordingly.

5. To serve, divide the hot meatballs among plates and garnish with the feta, tomatoes, cucumber, onion, and olives. Spoon some yogurt on each plate and sprinkle with the dill. Place a sprig of parsley and thyme on each plate.

YIELD: 6 SERVINGS
(24 TO 30 MEATBALLS)

2 teaspoons olive oil

⅓ cup finely chopped scallions

1 large clove garlic, minced

1 teaspoon salt

¾ teaspoon ground cinnamon

½ teaspoon ground cumin

¼ teaspoon ground allspice

1 pound ground lamb

¼ cup fine fresh bread crumbs

1 large egg, lightly beaten

Vegetable oil, for frying

4 ounces feta cheese, sliced

2 Roma tomatoes, chopped

1 medium cucumber, peeled, seeded, and chopped

¼ cup chopped red onion

¼ cup pitted Kalamata olives

¼ cup plain Greek yogurt

1 tablespoon minced fresh dill

6 fresh Italian parsley sprigs

6 fresh thyme sprigs

Mini Sliders

MINI BUNS

1½ cups warm water

¼ ounce (1 package) instant yeast

2 tablespoons molasses

2 tablespoons olive oil

4 cups all-purpose flour

1½ teaspoons salt

BEEF SLIDERS

Olive oil for the bowl

2 pounds ground beef

1 tablespoon ketchup

1 tablespoon Worcestershire sauce

1 large egg

1 tablespoon yellow mustard

1 teaspoon salt

¼ teaspoon freshly ground black pepper

4 tablespoons vegetable oil

These little burgers—beef and vegetarian—would make a nice pair on a plate as an appetizer, and would also satisfy a range of 'vores at a cocktail party.

1. Make the mini buns: Oil a bowl with olive oil and set aside. In the bowl of an electric mixer, combine all the remaining ingredients. The dough will remain a little sticky. Transfer the dough to a floured work surface and gently knead it into a soft ball. Put the dough in the oiled bowl and cover. Store in a warm, humid area for 30 minutes to 1 hour, or until the dough rises to double its size.

2. Preheat the oven to 400°F. Portion the dough into 1-inch round balls. Place the dough balls on a baking pan lined with parchment paper about 2 inches apart. Cover with plastic wrap and let the dough balls rise again, about 30 minutes. Bake the buns for 20 minutes, or until golden brown. Let cool on a wire rack. Split just before serving.

3. Make the beef sliders: In a large bowl, combine all the ingredients except the oil. With two forks, paw at the mixture until thoroughly combined.

4. Measure 2 to 3 tablespoons of the beef mixture and make a patty. Place the patty on a baking sheet and repeat with the remaining beef mixture. Cover and refrigerate until ready to cook and serve.

5. Make the vegetarian sliders: Bring a large pot of salted water to a boil and prepare a bowl of ice water. Add the green beans to the boiling water and cook until crisp-tender, 2 to 3 minutes (taste one—it should be just cooked through and tender). With a slotted spoon or strainer, remove the green beans and immediately put them in the bowl of ice water to stop the cooking. Transfer them from the ice water to a cutting board and dice them; put in a bowl. Repeat the process with the carrots and then the broccoli; add them both to the green beans. (The vegetables can be prepared to this point up to 4 hours ahead and refrigerated, covered.)

6. In a very large skillet, heat ¼ cup of the oil over medium-high heat. Add the onions and cook, stirring, for 2 minutes. Add the green beans, carrots, and broccoli; cook, stirring, until all the vegetables are tender, 5 to 8 minutes. Add the basil, thyme, and rosemary; cook, stirring, for 2 minutes.

7. Transfer the contents of the skillet to a blender or food processor and puree. (When pureeing hot ingredients, release one corner of the lid

to prevent a vacuum effect and place a kitchen towel over the top of the machine while you pulse.) With a rubber spatula, scrape the mixture into a large bowl and stir in the cheese, mashed potatoes, 1 cup of the panko, and 1 egg. Season with salt and pepper.

8. Shape the vegetable mixture into small patties. In a shallow bowl, beat the remaining 2 eggs. Put the flour and remaining 5 cups panko in separate shallow bowls. One by one, dredge each patty in the flour, then in the beaten eggs, and then in the panko. Place on a baking sheet and refrigerate until firm, about 1 hour.

9. Cook the beef and vegetable sliders: Preheat the oven to 180°F. In a large heavy skillet or cast-iron pan, heat 2 tablespoons vegetable oil over medium-high heat. Add a batch of beef patties to the pan (avoid overcrowding or they will steam rather than brown). Cook, turning once, until browned on both sides, 4 to 5 minutes total. With a slotted spoon, remove the patties and place on a clean baking sheet (top each patty with a cheese slice, if desired). Keep the finished patties warm in the oven while you cook the remaining patties, adding the remaining oil to the pan if necessary. Cook the vegetable patties in the same manner, using the remaining olive oil. Serve in the buns with a slice of tomato and onion and lettuce, if desired.

VEGETARIAN SLIDERS

8 ounces green beans, trimmed

8 ounces carrots, cut lengthwise and then into 2-inch pieces

8 ounces broccoli, separated into florets

½ cup olive oil

8 ounces onions, finely diced

½ cup chopped fresh basil, or 2 tablespoons dried basil

¼ cup chopped fresh thyme, or 1 tablespoon dried thyme

¼ cup chopped fresh rosemary, or 1 tablespoon dried rosemary

8 ounces Parmesan cheese, grated

4 ounces prepared mashed potatoes

6 cups (12 ounces) panko (Japanese bread crumbs)

3 large eggs

Salt and freshly ground black pepper

2 cups all-purpose flour

TOPPINGS (OPTIONAL)

30 small slices cheddar cheese

30 small slices tomato

30 small slices onion

30 small lettuce leaves

Prosciutto Parmesan Cracker Sticks

These little salty wands are fun to grab and delicious to crunch, especially when your other hand is holding a glass of wine.

1. Preheat the oven to 325°F. Line a baking sheet with parchment paper or a Silpat.
2. Remove the crusts from the bread and cut the bread into "sticks" measuring 4 inches by ½ inch by ½ inch. Generously brush the bread "sticks" with the clarified butter. Sprinkle the Parmesan onto a plate and dip the bread sticks into the Parmesan, coating them very well. Place them on the prepared baking sheet.
3. Bake for 4 to 6 minutes, until golden brown. Meanwhile, lay the prosciutto strips on a clean surface. When the bread sticks are finished baking, roll a prosciutto strip around one half of each stick. Serve with some Alfredo sauce or chutney for dipping, if desired.

> **NOTE** | To clarify butter, melt 1 cup (2 sticks) unsalted butter in a medium saucepan over low heat. Cook until the butterfat becomes clear and milk solids drop to the bottom of the pan. Skim the surface foam as the butter separates. Carefully spoon the clear butterfat into a measuring cup. Discard the milky liquid at the bottom of the saucepan.

YIELD: 2 TO 4 SERVINGS

2 to 3 large day-old French bread bâtons or mini baguettes

¼ cup clarified butter, warmed (see Note)

½ cup grated Parmesan cheese

4 slices prosciutto, each cut into four slices lengthwise

Alfredo sauce or chutney, for dipping (optional)

Tomato and Goat Cheese Tartlets

YIELD: 16 TARTLETS

1 (17.3-ounce) package frozen puff pastry (2 sheets), thawed

1 large egg, lightly beaten with 1 teaspoon water

6 Roma tomatoes, cut in half lengthwise

1 tablespoon herbes de Provence

Salt

Extra-virgin olive oil, for drizzling

3½ ounces ripened goat cheese, softened

½ cup purchased or homemade pesto

hile homemade puff pastry is delicious, it requires you to spend quite a bit of time waiting to repeat the rolling, folding, and chilling process over and over again. If you don't have that kind of time, frozen puff pastry is the perfect option. Unlike store-bought pie dough, frozen puff pastry closely resembles homemade in texture and often in flavor. Keep a box of frozen puff pastry in the freezer, and the time it takes to thaw it on the counter is all that stands between you and some elegant quick appetizers.

1. Line a large rimmed baking sheet with parchment paper. Roll out each puff pastry sheet on a lightly floured surface to make an 11-inch square. With a 2-½-inch round cutter or the rim of a wineglass, cut out 16 rounds from each pastry sheet, to make 32 rounds total. Place 16 rounds on the prepared baking sheet; pierce the rounds all over with a fork. Set aside.

2. With a 2-inch round cutter, cut out smaller rounds from the center of the remaining 16 rounds to make 16 (2½-inch) rings (reserve the 2-inch rounds for another use). Brush the outer ¼-inch edges of the 2½-inch rounds with some of the beaten egg; top each with 1 pastry ring. Freeze for at least 30 minutes. (The pastry can be prepared to this point up to 1 day ahead and frozen, covered. Do not thaw before continuing.)

3. Preheat the oven to 350°F. Line a baking sheet with foil. Place the tomato slices skin side down on a baking sheet and sprinkle with the herbes de Provence and salt. Drizzle with some oil and bake for 20 minutes, or until the tomatoes are softened and are almost beginning to brown. Remove the tomatoes from the oven and let them cool in the pan on a rack. Chop them into ¼-inch cubes and set aside.

4. Turn up the oven to 400°F. Place the chopped tomatoes inside the rings of the 16 frozen pastry rounds. Top the tomatoes with the goat cheese and bake for 10 minutes, or until the cheese is melted and the pastry is golden on the bottom and fully cooked. (If they still seem undercooked, switch off the oven and leave the pastries inside, with the oven door closed, for 3 to 4 minutes.) Serve warm, with a drizzle of pesto alongside.

Caprese Salad on a Stick

Because these skewers aren't grilled, use attractive bamboo knotted picks (or longer knotted skewers) for these fresh-tasting salad bites.

YIELD: 24 SKEWERS

24 (3- to 6-inch) bamboo picks or skewers

24 pieces of buffalo mozzarella cut to the size of the tomatoes

24 fresh basil leaves

24 grape or small cherry tomatoes, or larger heirloom tomatoes cut into 24 pieces

¼ cup balsamic vinegar

2 tablespoons extra-virgin olive oil

Salt and freshly ground black pepper

1. On each pick or skewer, thread a piece of mozzarella, a basil leaf, and a tomato (or piece of a tomato).
2. Put the vinegar in a small glass or ceramic bowl and slowly whisk in the oil. Season with salt and pepper.
3. Just before serving, roll each salad skewer in the balsamic mixture. Serve immediately.

Sweet Onion Tartlets

YIELD: 12 TARTLETS

2 tablespoons unsalted butter

1½ cups diced sweet onions

Salt and freshly ground black pepper

½ cup heavy cream

Pinch of freshly grated nutmeg

1 bunch scallions, white and light green parts only, coarsely chopped

1 medium red onion, cut into thin rings

1 large egg

12 mini phyllo shells (1½ inches in diameter) (see Note)

2 tablespoons grated Parmesan cheese

12 fresh chives

This tart with its colorful garnish shows off four kinds of onions against a simple creamy and crisp background.

1. Preheat the oven to 450°F. In a large skillet, heat 1 tablespoon of the butter over medium-high heat. Add the sweet onions and season with salt and pepper. Cook, stirring occasionally, until translucent, about 10 minutes. Add the cream and bring to a boil. Transfer the onion mixture to a bowl and season with the nutmeg and additional salt and pepper if needed; let cool to room temperature. (The mixture can be prepared to this point up to 1 day ahead and refrigerated, covered.)

2. For the garnish, heat the remaining 1 tablespoon butter in a skillet over medium heat. Add the scallions and red onion and cook, stirring, until soft and translucent, 3 to 4 minutes. Season with salt and pepper. Remove from the heat and set aside.

3. Lightly beat the egg and stir it into the sweet onion and cream mixture.

4. Fill each phyllo shell with some of the onion and cream mixture and top with a little Parmesan cheese. Bake for 7 to 10 minutes, until the tarts are lightly browned. Serve warm, garnished with the sautéed scallions and red onion and chives.

> **NOTE** If you can find phyllo sheets but not phyllo cups, butter 12 (½-cup) muffin cups and line each of them with 4 (6-inch) squares of phyllo, pressing them into the bottom and brushing with butter in between each square. Fold the pastry overhang inside, if you wish. Bake for about 10 minutes at 400°F until just golden. Let cool before using.

CHAPTER 6

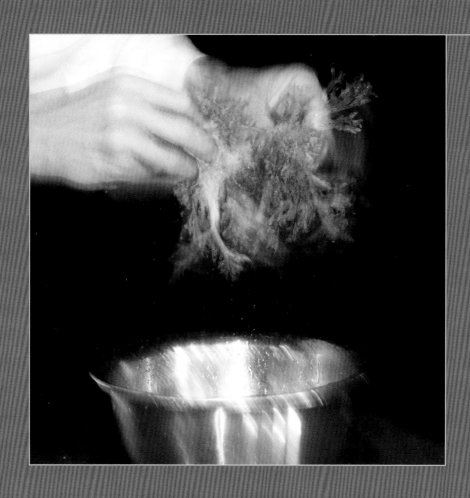

SALADS

Light appetizer salads have long been served as a sit-down starter to a meal to stimulate the appetite. I like to think of appetizer salads as also stimulating the imagination—bringing color and texture and structure together with bright refreshing flavors in combinations that ignite excitement at the table.

Salads offer an endless opportunity to express your creativity, both in the mix of ingredients and in the way you present them. I take great pleasure in building small appetizer salads that are as inspiring to the eye as they are pleasing to the palate.

Take the Master Chef Mini Salad Bouquet: Thinking about salad as a beautiful bouquet totally transforms the presentation into a dish almost too lovely to eat. (Holland America Line guests often discreetly pull out their phones during dinner to take a picture of this dish!)

The appetizer portion size truly allows you to be playful with any of these salads and really mix things up. I'm fond of serving the Shrimp and Crab Louie in an elegant stemmed martini glass. Have a set of great dramatic small rice bowls in your china cabinet? They might be a perfect way to show off the spicy Thai Green Papaya Salad. Each of these salads lends itself to a special visual presentation.

A starter salad is a perfect way to hint at the style and promise of what's to come. If you are planning a meal with a decided sense of luxury, start it with the Lobster Salad on Artichokes. If a hearty warming roast is on the menu, consider starting with a more rustic, homey salad like the Creamy and Crunchy Cauliflower and Radish Salad. Need a wonderful start to your Thanksgiving feast? Try the beautiful Roasted Beets with Frisée, Blue Cheese, and Sweet and Spicy Pecans for a delicious beginning. No matter what's on the menu, you'll find an ideal appetizer salad from this collection of Holland America Line favorites.

Master Chef Mini Salad Bouquet

S alad bouquets look beautiful and appetizing, whether they're in a tomato "vase" or tucked inside a hollowed-out ring of toasted baguette. Here's a mini version, where thin zucchini strips keep the salad elevated and elegant.

1. Make the red pepper dressing: With a mortar and pestle, mash the red pepper with the garlic and a pinch of salt and pepper. When the mixture is smooth, scrape it into a medium bowl. Whisk in the egg yolk, mustard, and vinegar. Very slowly whisk in the olive oil, then the peanut oil. Adjust the seasonings. (There will be more dressing than you need for the salad bouquet. Cover and refrigerate the remaining dressing for up to 2 days.)

2. Make the salad bouquets: Wrap 1 or 2 strips of zucchini loosely around the neck of a bottle of olive oil to form a ring. Slide the zucchini ring off the bottle and secure with a toothpick. Repeat to make 4 rings. Set aside.

3. With your fingers, make 4 bouquets of the lettuces and bell peppers. Tuck the bouquets into the rings, adjusting the ring size if necessary.

4. To serve, ladle some dressing onto a small rimmed plate. Stand the salad bouquet in the center and serve immediately.

NOTE You can eliminate the small risk of salmonella contamination in raw egg preparations by using pasteurized shell eggs.

YIELD: 4 SERVINGS

RED PEPPER DRESSING

1 tablespoon minced roasted red pepper, from a jar or homemade (see page 20)

1 clove garlic, minced

Salt and freshly ground black pepper

1 large egg yolk, at room temperature (see Note)

1 tablespoon Dijon mustard, at room temperature

1 tablespoon red wine vinegar

½ cup extra-virgin olive oil

½ cup peanut oil

SALAD BOUQUETS

1 zucchini, trimmed and cut into lengthwise slices with a mandoline slicer (see Note, page 70)

4 decorative toothpicks

4 leaves green leaf lettuce

4 leaves radicchio or red oak lettuce

8 leaves frisée

½ medium red bell pepper, cut into ¼-inch strips

½ medium green bell pepper, cut into ¼-inch strips

½ medium orange bell pepper, cut into ¼-inch strips

½ medium yellow bell pepper, cut into ¼-inch strips

Roasted Beets with Frisée, Blue Cheese, and Sweet and Spicy Pecans

BALSAMIC VINAIGRETTE

½ cup balsamic vinegar

2 tablespoons Dijon mustard

1 tablespoon sugar

1 teaspoon salt

1 teaspoon freshly ground black pepper

1 tablespoon minced shallot

¼ cup olive oil

½ cup canola oil (or other vegetable oil)

SWEET AND SPICY PECANS

1 large egg white

3 tablespoons sugar

½ teaspoon ground cinnamon (optional)

Cayenne pepper or freshly ground black pepper

1 cup pecan halves

SALAD

1 pound beets, trimmed with 1 inch of stems still attached, scrubbed (see Note)

2 cups frisée

4 to 5 ounces blue cheese

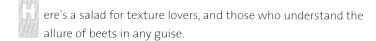

ere's a salad for texture lovers, and those who understand the allure of beets in any guise.

1. Make the balsamic vinaigrette: In a glass or ceramic bowl, combine the vinegar, mustard, sugar, salt, pepper, and shallot. Whisk until the sugar is dissolved. Slowly whisk in the olive oil, then the canola oil. Cover and refrigerate the vinaigrette until ready to use.

2. Make the sweet and spicy pecans: Preheat the oven to 350°F. Line a baking sheet with parchment paper.

3. In a medium bowl, whisk the egg white until slightly frothy. Whisk in the sugar, cinnamon (if using), and cayenne pepper. With a rubber spatula, stir in the pecans, tossing until well coated.

4. Spread the pecans on the prepared baking sheet in a single layer and bake for 10 to 15 minutes, until dry and toasted (check them frequently so they don't burn). Transfer to a plate and let cool.

5. Make the salad: Preheat the oven to 425°F. Tightly wrap the beets in double layers of heavy-duty foil and roast on a baking sheet placed on the middle rack of the oven until they are tender and a small knife easily pierces the flesh, 30 to 45 minutes for smaller beets, 1 to 1½ hours for larger beets. Let cool in the foil until warm, about 20 minutes.

6. When the beets are cool enough to handle, peel them, discarding the stems and root ends. Cut them crosswise into ¼-inch-thick slices, then into sticks, then into cubes. Place in a glass or ceramic bowl and toss with just enough of the vinaigrette to lightly coat the beets.

7. To serve, divide the frisée among the plates and top with the beets. Drizzle the frisée and greens with some of the vinaigrette and top with some blue cheese. Sprinkle with the pecans and serve immediately.

> **NOTE** Raw beets will keep for a few weeks, sealed in a plastic bag in the refrigerator. If you bought beets with greens attached, remove them before storing the beets, but don't throw them out! They're packed with nutrients and are delicious, but should be cooked soon after purchase. Just rinse them, cut them into ribbons, and sauté them in butter or olive oil with salt and pepper.

Apple, Pear, and Cucumber Salad

hough it positively sings with holiday spirit, this salad is wonderful any time of year when you'd love some crisp flavors and textures.

1. Make the lemon vinaigrette: In a small glass or ceramic bowl, whisk together the lemon juice and shallot. Slowly whisk in the oil. Stir in the chives. Season with salt and white pepper. Cover and refrigerate until ready to use.

2. Make the salad: In a glass or ceramic bowl, combine the dried cherries, orange juice concentrate, and cranberry juice. Let steep for 30 minutes. Add the apple, pear, cucumber, and red onion. Toss to combine.

3. Preheat the oven to 350°F. In a small bowl, combine the oil, butter, and salt. Brush the baguette slices all over with the butter mixture and place on a baking sheet. Bake for 8 minutes. Remove the slices from the oven and top each with a sprinkling of the cheese. Return to the oven until the cheese is melted and the bread slices are golden, about 2 minutes longer.

4. In a large bowl, toss the lettuces with just enough of the vinaigrette to lightly coat the leaves. Divide among serving plates and top with a mound of the apple mixture. Crown the apple mixture with a gorgonzola crouton and serve immediately.

YIELD: 6 SERVINGS

LEMON VINAIGRETTE

2 tablespoons fresh lemon juice (from about 1 lemon)

1 teaspoon minced shallot

½ cup extra-virgin olive oil

2 teaspoons minced fresh chives

Salt

Freshly ground white pepper

SALAD

¾ cup dried cherries

2 tablespoons orange juice concentrate

2 tablespoons cranberry juice

¾ cup peeled and diced apple

¾ cup peeled and diced pear

¾ cup peeled and diced English (seedless) cucumber

3 tablespoons minced red onion

2 tablespoons extra-virgin olive oil

1 tablespoon butter, melted

Pinch of salt

6 (½-inch-thick) slices of baguette

3 ounces gorgonzola cheese, crumbled

12 ounces baby frisée

6 butter lettuce leaves

6 radicchio leaves

Thai Green Papaya Salad

YIELD: 4 TO 6 SERVINGS

3 tablespoons dried shrimp (see Note)

Scant ½ cup fresh lime juice

2 tablespoons fish sauce (see Note)

2½ tablespoons honey

1 tablespoon palm sugar (see Note)

Scant ½ cup olive oil

2½ pounds green papaya, peeled, seeded, and coarsely shredded using the largest holes on a grater

¾ cup fresh bean sprouts

1 fresh plum tomato, seeded and cut into thin strips

5 medium scallions, white and light green parts only, sliced into thin strips

2 tablespoons seeded Thai chiles or serrano chiles sliced into thin strips

3 tablespoons roughly chopped fresh Thai basil leaves (see Note)

⅔ cup chopped honey-roasted peanuts

3 tablespoons roughly chopped fresh cilantro leaves

reen papaya has a slightly tart flavor, which complements the spicy, salty, and sweet flavors of this salad perfectly. It's delicious as a side dish as well as a starter.

1. Crush the dried shrimp in a mortar and pestle, then transfer to a glass or ceramic bowl. Add the lime juice, fish sauce, honey, and palm sugar, stirring to combine. Slowly whisk in the oil. Cover and refrigerate the dressing until ready to use.

2. In a large bowl, combine the green papaya, bean sprouts, tomato, scallions, chiles, and 2 tablespoons of the basil. Toss the mixture with just enough of the dressing to lightly coat it. Add the peanuts and toss again. Divide among plates and sprinkle with the remaining 1 tablespoon basil and the cilantro.

NOTE Dried shrimp, fish sauce, palm sugar, and Thai basil are available at Asian grocery stores.

Shrimp and Crab Louie

DRESSING

½ cup mayonnaise, store-bought or homemade (page 27)

¼ cup ketchup

¼ cup Thousand Island dressing, store-bought or homemade (recipe follows)

1 roasted red bell pepper, minced

6 Kalamata (or other black) olives, pitted and minced

1 tablespoon sweet relish

1 tablespoon fresh lemon juice

2 teaspoons Worcestershire sauce

1 teaspoon Tabasco sauce

SALAD

½ cup very thinly sliced romaine lettuce

⅓ cup very thinly sliced iceberg lettuce

⅓ cup finely grated carrot

⅓ cup very thinly sliced radicchio

⅓ cup very thinly sliced red cabbage

6 ounces jumbo lump crabmeat

2 large eggs, hard cooked, peeled, and finely chopped

18 medium or large shrimp (about 12 ounces), cooked, peeled, and chilled

6 lime wedges

6 frisée leaves

For a little taste of the past, serve this salad, from a century-old American recipe, in a martini glass, with shrimp crowning the top for added elegance.

1. Make the dressing: In a glass or ceramic bowl, whisk together all the ingredients. Cover and refrigerate until ready to use.
2. Make the salad: In a large bowl, combine the lettuces, carrot, radicchio, and cabbage. Toss gently until well combined and divide among 6 chilled martini glasses.
3. Remove any stray bits of shell or cartilage from the crabmeat, keeping the lumps intact. In a bowl, gently combine the crab with just enough dressing to coat. Place some crab on the lettuce in each Martini glass and sprinkle with chopped eggs. Top each salad with 2 shrimp and garnish with a lime wedge and a leaf of frisée.

THOUSAND ISLAND DRESSING

1¼ cups mayonnaise, store-bought or homemade (page 27)

⅓ cup chili sauce (a sweet rather than spicy variety)

¼ cup finely chopped roasted red bell peppers (see page 20)

3 tablespoons finely chopped sour cornichons or dill pickle

1 tablespoon Dijon mustard

2 tablespoons drained and finely chopped capers

2 tablespoons minced fresh chives

Salt and freshly ground black pepper

Tabasco sauce

In a glass or ceramic bowl, combine the mayonnaise, chili sauce, red pepper, cornichons, mustard, capers, and chives. Season with salt, pepper, and Tabasco. Cover and refrigerate until ready to serve. YIELD: 2 CUPS

Mediterranean Seafood Salad

7 ounces black mussels, scrubbed and debearded

2 teaspoons unsalted butter

4 ounces bay scallops, side muscle removed

4 ounces squid, cooked and diced

Salt

½ red bell pepper, cut into ⅛-inch pieces

½ green bell pepper, cut into ⅛-inch pieces

10 Kalamata olives and/or green olives, pitted

½ cup peeled, seeded, and diced tomato (see page 111)

2 teaspoons minced fresh parsley, plus 10 sprigs for garnish

1 teaspoon minced fresh oregano

2 teaspoons fresh lemon juice

2 teaspoons white wine

2 teaspoons Dijon mustard

½ teaspoon crushed red pepper

1 tablespoon plus 1 teaspoon extra-virgin olive oil

Freshly ground black pepper

10 Boston lettuce leaves or endive leaves

½ pound cooked asparagus spears (optional)

¼ cup diced seeded cucumber

10 lemon wedges

½ pound jumbo shrimp, cooked and peeled (see Note)

ake this delicious and colorful appetizer in advance to allow the bright flavors to mingle.

1. In a saucepan, bring ½ cup water and the mussels (in their shells) to a boil. Reduce the heat, cover, and simmer the mussels until they open, 4 to 5 minutes. Using tongs, transfer the mussels to a medium bowl (discard any that remain closed after cooking). Pull the mussels from their shells and place them in a bowl. Cover and refrigerate until well chilled, about 2 hours. (The mussels can be prepared 1 day ahead. Keep refrigerated.)

2. In a skillet, heat the butter over high heat. Add the scallops and sauté until cooked through, 4 to 5 minutes. Transfer the scallops to a large glass or ceramic bowl. Cover and refrigerate until well chilled, about 2 hours. (The scallops can be prepared 1 day ahead. Keep refrigerated.)

3. Rinse the squid under cold running water, then pat dry between paper towels. Halve the tentacles lengthwise and cut the bodies (including flaps, if attached) into ¼-inch dice. Bring 3 quarts water and 1 tablespoon salt to a boil over high heat. Prepare a bowl of ice water. Add squid to the boiling water and cook, uncovered, until just opaque, 30 to 40 seconds. Drain and immediately transfer the squid to an ice bath to stop the cooking. When the squid is cool, drain and pat dry and place in a bowl.

4. In a large glass or ceramic bowl, combine the mussels, scallops, squid, bell peppers, olives, tomato, minced parsley, and oregano; set aside. In a small bowl, combine the lemon juice, wine, mustard,

NOTE To cook shrimp, buy shell-on large- to jumbo-size shrimp (they can be purchased deveined) and add them to a pot of boiling salted water. Cook, stirring occasionally, for 2 to 3 minutes, until the shrimp are no longer raw in the middle (test by cutting into one shrimp after 2 minutes). Don't overcook. Remove the shrimp and plunge them into ice water to stop the cooking. Drain immediately. Peel—leaving the tail shells on if you wish—and set aside, covered, in the refrigerator, until ready to serve.

and crushed red pepper. Slowly whisk the oil into the lemon mixture. Season with salt and pepper. Drizzle the lemon dressing over the seafood mixture. With a rubber spatula, gently fold together until coated. Cover and refrigerate for 4 to 6 hours to let the flavors marinate.

5. To serve, line chilled plates with the lettuce leaves. Spoon some seafood salad onto the lettuce and garnish with the asparagus spears (if using), cucumber, lemon wedges, and parsley sprigs. Top each salad with some shrimp and serve immediately.

Roast Beef and Celery Root Salad with Tomato Apple Relish

he recipe for the homey tomato apple relish that tops the beef and celery root salad makes about 2 pints; it's more than you need for the salad, but the relish, which will keep for about a month in the refrigerator, is handy to have around for serving with meat loaf, roast pork, or baked beans.

1. In a glass or ceramic bowl, whisk the mayonnaise, sour cream, horseradish, Worcestershire sauce, mustard, and lemon juice. Add the celery root and toss until well coated. Season with salt and pepper. Gently fold in the roast beef and romaine.

2. Position a 1½-inch-high ring mold on a plate and fill almost to the top with the beef salad mixture. Top with a layer of tomato apple relish and carefully remove the ring. Place some red oak lettuce leaves on top. Repeat with the remaining salad, relish, and lettuce on the remaining plates.

3. To serve, spoon a line of tomato apple relish alongside the salad, garnish with a chive strand, and serve immediately.

TOMATO APPLE RELISH

In a heavy 4-quart pot, combine all the ingredients and bring to a boil over high heat, stirring occasionally. Reduce the heat to medium-low and cook, stirring occasionally, until the mixture is thick and the liquid has been absorbed, about 1 hour. Transfer the relish to a glass container and let cool. Cover and refrigerate until ready to use. (The relish will keep, covered, in the refrigerator for up to 1 month.) YIELD: ABOUT 2 PINTS

> **NOTE** To peel and seed tomatoes, use a paring knife to cut out the stems from the tomatoes and make a small X in the opposite ends. Plunge the tomatoes into boiling water and leave them in just until the skins are loosened, 10 to 20 seconds. With a slotted spoon, transfer the tomatoes to a bowl of cold water to cool. Slip off the skins. To seed: Cut the tomatoes in half along the equator. Gently but firmly squeeze the seeds from the halves. Now you're ready to chop or dice.

YIELD: 10 SERVINGS

2 tablespoons mayonnaise, store-bought or homemade (page 27)

2 tablespoons sour cream

1 teaspoon bottled horseradish, drained

½ teaspoon Worcestershire sauce

½ teaspoon Dijon mustard

⅛ teaspoon fresh lemon juice

1 pound celery root (celeriac), trimmed, peeled, and cut into thin strips (or grated on a box grater)

Salt and freshly ground black pepper

1¾ pounds medium-rare roast beef, cut into thin strips

10 romaine leaves, chopped

Tomato Apple Relish (recipe follows)

10 baby red oak lettuce leaves

10 fresh chives

TOMATO APPLE RELISH

2½ pounds tomatoes, peeled, seeded, and coarsely chopped (3 cups; see Note)

2 sweet apples, peeled, cored, and coarsely chopped

2 cups finely diced onion

1 green bell pepper, finely diced

1 red bell pepper, finely diced

½ cup raisins

½ cup apple cider vinegar

½ cup tightly packed brown sugar

1½ teaspoons black mustard seeds

½ teaspoon salt

½ teaspoon turmeric

¼ teaspoon celery seeds

Lobster Salad on Artichokes

4 large artichokes

1 lemon, halved crosswise

3 tablespoons all-purpose flour

2 tablespoons olive oil

1 tablespoon red wine vinegar

1 teaspoon Dijon mustard

2 tablespoons heavy cream

¼ teaspoon salt

⅛ teaspoon freshly ground black pepper

8 ounces cooked lobster meat, chilled and cut into ½-inch chunks

8 Boston lettuce leaves, washed in cold water and drained

1 tablespoon chopped fresh chives

I n salads, lobster partners well with smooth ingredients. Avocado is a common lobster salad component, but artichoke is also delicious, with the added benefit that fresh artichokes contain cynarin, which makes your taste buds recognize sweetness in the foods paired with them.

1. Twist the stems off the artichokes and snap off the outside leaves by bending them backward. (Leave the bunch of yellowish leaves in the center of the artichoke intact.) Cut off the top two thirds of the artichoke, leaving only the flat base. Trim away any vestiges of tough outer leaves and trim the artichoke bottom into a smooth round. Constantly rub the artichoke with the lemon halves while trimming to prevent discoloration.

2. Fill a large saucepan with 1 gallon salted water. In a small bowl, combine the flour with enough water to make a sauce consistency. Pour this mixture into the 1 gallon water and whisk to combine. Place the saucepan over medium heat, squeeze the lemon halves into the water, and bring to a boil.

3. Add the artichokes to the saucepan and boil until you can easily pierce the bottoms with a knife, about 20 minutes. (The larger the artichokes, the more time it will take to cook them.) Drain them upside down in a colander.

4. In a medium bowl, whisk the oil, vinegar, mustard, cream, salt, and pepper. With a rubber spatula, gently fold in the lobster until combined. To serve, place an artichoke heart on each plate and line it with some lettuce. Divide the lobster salad among the artichoke hearts. Sprinkle with the chives and serve immediately.

Creamy and Crunchy Cauliflower and Radish Salad

Cauliflower and radishes are at peak season at the same time, and make an interesting texture contrast with the creamy yogurt dressing.

1. Cook the cauliflower in a large saucepan of boiling salted water until just tender, about 2 minutes. Drain and let cool. Transfer to a bowl and add the radishes.

2. In a dry skillet over high heat, toss or stir the sesame seeds, taking care not to scorch them, until lightly browned. Transfer them to a small bowl and let cool.

3. In another small bowl, combine the yogurt, tahini, and honey. Season with salt and pepper. Pour over the cauliflower mixture and gently toss to coat.

4. To serve, line each plate with some lettuce and top with some cauliflower and radish salad. Sprinkle with the toasted sesame seeds and chives and serve.

YIELD: 6 SERVINGS

1 head cauliflower, broken into small florets

Salt

1 bunch radishes, trimmed and quartered

2 teaspoons sesame seeds

⅔ cup plain yogurt

4 teaspoons tahini (sesame seed paste)

1 teaspoon honey

Freshly ground black pepper

6 to 12 Boston lettuce leaves

Chives, for garnish

Endive and Orange Salad with Hazelnut Dressing

HAZELNUT DRESSING

3 tablespoons hazelnut oil

3 tablespoons fresh orange juice (reserved from oranges in salad below)

Pinch of apple pie spice

Salt and freshly ground black pepper

SALAD

½ cup hazelnuts

4 heads green and purple Belgian endive, chopped, plus 10 to 12 whole leaves for garnish

3 oranges, peel and pith removed, fruit cut into segments, juices reserved

1 tablespoon chopped fresh parsley

or many salads, a trio of flavors is just right. Here, the sweetness of the oranges counters the bitter endive. The hazelnuts provide crunch, an earthy undertone, and additional subtle sweetness.

1. Make the hazelnut dressing: In a small glass or ceramic bowl, combine the oil, orange juice, and apple pie spice. Season with salt and pepper. Set aside.

2. Make the salad: Preheat the oven to 350°F. Spread the hazelnuts on a baking sheet and bake for 10 to 15 minutes, until pale golden beneath the skins. Let cool briefly, then rub inside a clean kitchen towel to remove as much of the skins as possible. Coarsely chop the nuts and set aside.

3. Place the chopped endive in a glass or ceramic bowl. Cut the orange segments in half and add them to the endive. Pour the dressing over the salad and toss to coat. Transfer to a serving bowl and sprinkle with the hazelnuts. Garnish with the whole endive leaves and parsley and serve.

CHAPTER 7

ANTIPASTO AND MEZE ASSORTMENTS

With dozens of spectacular Mediterranean cruises running every year, I couldn't resist devoting a whole chapter to the special appetizer preparations made famous by the region—antipasto and meze.

Like the Mediterranean destinations from which they hail, antipasto and meze platters always offer something for everyone, wonderful prepared vegetables in bite-sized servings, delicious cured meats, savory dips and spreads, crusty breads, smoked fish, rich dried fruits and refreshing fresh fruits, flavorful vinegars and oils, mushrooms, eggs, fresh herbs, and on and on. In short, antipasto and meze platters are surefire crowd pleasers.

From the perspective of the cook, serving an antipasto or meze plate gives you wonderful flexibility and great opportunities to create stunning presentations. In this collection of recipes, you'll find many mini recipes that make up the whole dish as we would typically present it as a precursor to a meal or during a cocktail party on board our ships. But I encourage you to create your own signature antipasto presentations by mixing and matching any of these recipes.

Undoubtedly, you'll also find a number of them that will become personal favorites, either as stand-alone appetizers, such as the delicious Baba Ghanoush, Hummus, or Spanish Serrano Ham with Pickled Grilled Asparagus, or as a side dish to accompany your main course, like the Marinated Vegetables or the Tabbouleh.

Truly, you'll be able to capture the romance of the Mediterranean with these wonderful dishes—and you'll be able to take your guests along for the journey in great taste and style.

Spanish Serrano Ham with Pickled Grilled Asparagus

YIELD: 6 SERVINGS

1 cup sugar

1 cup distilled white vinegar

4 whole black peppercorns

1 bay leaf

1½ pounds standard or large (not jumbo) asparagus, tough skin peeled from lower inch

2 tablespoons plus ¼ cup extra-virgin olive oil

Salt and freshly ground black pepper

1½ pounds seeded and finely chopped tomatoes (about 2½ cups)

¾ cup black olives, pitted and sliced, plus 18 whole pitted olives for garnish

½ cup finely chopped red onion

2 tablespoons balsamic vinegar

2 tablespoons Worcestershire sauce

2 tablespoons finely chopped fresh basil, plus 6 whole sprigs for garnish

6 to 12 green or purple endive leaves

8 ounces thinly sliced Serrano ham (see Note)

S weet and tangy pickled grilled asparagus combines deliciously with a deep-flavored Spanish ham. A tangy and salty tomato and olive salad echoes the flavors and brings it all together.

1. In a medium saucepan, combine the sugar, white vinegar, ½ cup water, the peppercorns, and bay leaf. Bring the mixture to a boil and stir until the sugar has fully dissolved. Remove from the heat and let cool.

2. Preheat a charcoal, gas, or electric grill to medium-hot (when you can hold your hand 5 inches above the rack for 3 to 4 seconds). Drizzle the asparagus with 2 tablespoons of the oil and season with salt and pepper. Grill the asparagus until crisp-tender, turning occasionally, about 6 minutes. (Alternatively, cook the asparagus in a hot grill pan on the stovetop for about 4 minutes on each side.) Transfer the asparagus to a glass or ceramic baking dish. Pour the white vinegar mixture over the asparagus and marinate for 2 hours, or until it has a sweet pickled flavor.

3. In a medium glass or ceramic bowl, combine the tomatoes, chopped olives, and onion. In a smaller bowl, combine the balsamic vinegar and Worcestershire sauce. Slowly whisk in the remaining ¼ cup oil. Stir in the chopped basil. Gently fold just enough of the dressing into the tomato mixture to lightly coat.

4. To serve, spoon some tomato relish in the front of each plate. Wrap the bottom of some endive leaves with some Serrano ham slices and place them behind the relish. Drape some pickled asparagus spears on the relish and garnish the plate with the whole olives and basil sprig. Serve immediately.

NOTE   Serrano ham is a country ham produced in Spain. Cured with sea salt and dried for a year to eighteen months, Serrano has a deep flavor and aroma that's different from prosciutto, which is cured a shorter time with a coating of lard and has more fat. Serrano is firmer than prosciutto, but can still be thinly sliced.

Captain's Antipasto Plate

YIELD: 5 SERVINGS

MARINATED VEGETABLES

1¼ cups white wine vinegar

1¼ cups plus 2 tablespoons extra-virgin olive oil

¼ to ½ bunch fresh rosemary (about 15 sprigs), leaves finely chopped

10 asparagus spears, tough skin peeled from lower inch

Salt and freshly ground black pepper

6 tablespoons fresh lemon juice

1 pound button mushrooms, stems trimmed flush with caps

1 (14-ounce) can artichoke hearts in brine, drained and lightly rinsed

ANTIPASTO

3 large or 5 small loaves Italian bread (optional)

2 tablespoons olive oil

8 ounces small mozzarella balls (*ciliegine*)

10 sour cornichons

10 (¼-inch-thick) slices country pâté

10 very thin slices prosciutto, rolled into individual bunches (about 3 ounces)

4 ounces thinly sliced bresaola (air-dried salted beef)

5 cherry tomatoes or small tomatoes, cut in half

4 ounces thinly sliced coppa pork

Basil Dressing (page 125)

5 fresh rosemary sprigs

5 fresh basil sprigs

1 head oak leaf lettuce (optional)

This meat-laden plate is a Holland America Line signature. Cured beef and pork products share equal billing with a trio of separately marinated Mediterranean-style vegetables. As with all antipasto recipes, always try to create an exciting presentation that emphasizes *abbodanza* ("abundance" in Italian).

1. Make the marinated vegetables: In a 4-cup glass measuring cup, whisk the vinegar, 1¼ cups of the oil, and the rosemary. Set the marinade aside.
2. Preheat a charcoal, gas, or electric grill to medium-hot (when you can hold your hand 5 inches above the rack for 3 to 4 seconds). Drizzle the asparagus with 1 tablespoon of the remaining oil and season with salt and pepper. Grill the asparagus until crisp-tender, turning occasionally, about 6 minutes. (Alternatively, cook the asparagus in a hot grill pan on the stovetop for about 4 minutes on each side.) Transfer the asparagus to a glass or ceramic baking dish and sprinkle with 2 tablespoons of the lemon juice. Add ¾ cup of the marinade and set aside to marinate for 1 to 2 hours.
3. Drizzle the mushrooms with the remaining 1 tablespoon oil and season with salt and pepper. Grill the mushrooms until lightly browned and tender, about 10 minutes. (If the mushrooms are small, grill them on skewers or on a lightly oiled perforated grill sheet.) Cut the mushrooms in half (if large) and transfer them to a glass or ceramic bowl; sprinkle with 2 tablespoons of the lemon juice. Add ¾ cup of the marinade and set aside to marinate for 1 to 2 hours.
4. Cut the drained and rinsed artichoke hearts into quarters and place in a glass or ceramic bowl. Sprinkle with the remaining 2 tablespoons lemon juice and season with salt and pepper. Add ¾ cup of the marinade and set aside to marinate for 1 to 2 hours. (Divide any remaining marinade among the vegetables or store it, covered, in the refrigerator for up to 4 days for another use.)
5. Make the antipasto: If serving the antipasto on bread, preheat the broiler. Slice the top off the bread (save for another use) and spread the remaining flat slice with some of the oil. Broil the bread until just starting to turn golden. Remove from the oven and place on a tray (if using 3 loaves) or plates (if serving individually).

6. Place the mozzarella, cornichons, and pâté on the bread. On top, place side-by-side the prosciutto, asparagus, mushrooms, bresaola, tomatoes, artichokes, and coppa. Spoon some basil dressing over all and garnish with the rosemary and basil sprigs.

7. If serving the antipasto on lettuce, line each plate (or a large tray) with lettuce and spoon the drained artichokes and drained mushrooms in the center. Surround the marinated vegetables with the pâté, coppa, bresaola, and prosciutto, separately bunched or bundled. Drape the asparagus over the top. Spoon some basil dressing over all and garnish with the rosemary and basil sprigs.

Heirloom Tomatoes and Ciliegine with Toasted Focaccia

iliegine is fresh mozzarella in the shape of small, cherry-sized balls. (*Bocconcini* are slightly larger.) If *ciliegine* are unavailable, substitute 1-inch cubes of fresh mozzarella. This appetizer is the simplest antipasto assortment there is, and it sings of summer and freshness.

1. Make the basil dressing: In a food processor, combine the basil, garlic, and salt; blend to a coarse puree. With the machine running, gradually blend in the oil. Transfer to a bowl and cover tightly until ready to use. (The dressing keeps, refrigerated, for up to 6 hours. Store any leftover dressing, covered, in the freezer to add flavor to soups or pasta dishes.)

2. Make the tomatoes and *ciliegine*: Preheat a charcoal, gas, or electric grill to medium-hot (when you can hold your hand 5 inches above the rack for 3 to 4 seconds). Brush the focaccia on both sides with oil and lightly season with salt and pepper. Grill the focaccia until lightly toasted, 1 to 3 minutes on each side, rotating it 90 degrees about halfway through to give it attractive grill marks. Cut each focaccia square in half into triangles. (Alternatively, grill the focaccia in a hot grill pan on the stove for 2 to 4 minutes on each side.)

3. Line the serving plates with the lettuce. Arrange the tomatoes and *ciliegine* on each plate and drizzle with some of the dressing. Season lightly with salt and pepper. Garnish with the basil sprigs and serve immediately with a focaccia triangle.

NOTE | Focaccia and ciabatta are Italian flatbreads available in many bakeries and supermarkets.

YIELD: 6 SERVINGS

BASIL DRESSING

8 ounces fresh basil, stemmed and cut into strips (for easier processing)

½ teaspoon minced garlic

¼ teaspoon salt

½ cup extra-virgin olive oil

TOMATOES AND *CILIEGINE*

3 (4-inch) squares of focaccia or ciabatta bread (see Note)

¼ cup olive oil

Salt and freshly ground black pepper

12 Boston lettuce leaves

3 heirloom tomatoes, peeled and cut into eighths (see Note, page 111)

1 pound small mozzarella balls (*ciliegine*)

6 fresh basil sprigs

Meze Plate

YIELD: 10 SERVINGS

BABA GHANOUSH

1 tablespoon olive oil

1 large eggplant (about 1½ pounds)

¼ cup tahini (sesame seed paste)

3 tablespoons fresh lemon juice

2½ teaspoons minced garlic

Salt and freshly ground black pepper

3 tablespoons chopped fresh flat-leaf parsley

STUFFED GRAPE LEAVES

½ cup olive oil

6 scallions, chopped

¾ cup long-grain white rice

⅔ cup fresh lemon juice

¼ cup chopped fresh mint

2 tablespoons chopped fresh dill

1 tablespoon tomato paste

½ teaspoon ground allspice

Salt and freshly ground black pepper

¼ cup dried currants

¼ cup pine nuts

1 (8-ounce) jar grape leaves, drained and rinsed

HUMMUS

1 (15-ounce) can chickpeas (garbanzo beans), drained

3 tablespoons extra-virgin olive oil

3 tablespoons tahini (sesame seed paste)

1 clove garlic, chopped

Juice of 1 lemon

Salt and freshly ground black pepper

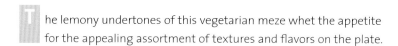

he lemony undertones of this vegetarian meze whet the appetite for the appealing assortment of textures and flavors on the plate.

1. Make the baba ghanoush: Preheat the oven to 450°F. Brush a baking sheet with the oil.

2. Cut the eggplant in half lengthwise and place cut side down on the prepared baking sheet. Roast for 1 to 1½ hours, until the skin is charred and the interior is fully cooked. Let the eggplant stand until cool enough to handle.

3. Scrape the eggplant pulp into a blender (discard the skin). Add the tahini, lemon juice, and garlic. Blend until smooth. Season with salt and pepper. Add 2 teaspoons water and the parsley; pulse just until combined. Transfer the baba ghanoush to a glass or ceramic bowl, cover, and refrigerate until ready to use.

4. Make the stuffed grape leaves: In a medium saucepan, heat ¼ cup of the oil over medium heat. Add the scallions and cook, stirring, for 1 minute. Add the rice, ⅓ cup of the lemon juice, the mint, dill, tomato paste, and allspice. Stir briefly to combine. Season with salt and pepper. Add 1 cup water and bring to a boil. Reduce the heat to low, cover, and simmer for 10 to 15 minutes, until the rice is almost cooked.

5. Remove the rice from the heat. With a fork, gently stir in the currants and pine nuts until just combined. Let cool.

6. Place a grape leaf shiny side down on a work surface. Spoon 1 tablespoon of the rice mixture into the center of the leaf. With the stem end of the leaf closest to you, fold the sides of the leaf toward the center and roll the filling into the leaf tightly so it resembles a cigar. Repeat with the remaining leaves and rice mixture.

7. Make a thin layer of some broken or too-small grape leaves in the bottom of a 3-quart saucepan and arrange the stuffed grape leaves closely together in the base of the pan, and in another layer if necessary. Pour in the remaining ⅓ cup lemon juice, the remaining

(See photograph page 185)

¼ cup oil, and enough water to just cover the stuffed grape leaves. Invert a plate onto the grape leaves to hold them down and put a heavy can on the plate to compress them slightly and keep them in place while they cook.

8. Bring to a boil. Immediately reduce the heat to low and simmer for 45 minutes (add more water if necessary so the bottom of the pan doesn't dry out). Remove from the heat and let cool in the pan. Serve at room temperature. (The stuffed grape leaves can be made in advance and refrigerated, covered, for up to 2 weeks.)

9. Make the hummus: In a blender or food processor, combine the chickpeas, oil, tahini, garlic, and lemon juice. Process until smooth. Season with salt and pepper. Transfer to a bowl, cover, and refrigerate until ready to serve.

10. Make the tabbouleh: In a medium skillet, heat 1 tablespoon of the oil over medium heat. Add the bulgur and toast, stirring constantly, until fragrant, about 2 minutes. Add the boiling water and bring to a simmer. Reduce the heat and simmer for 1 minute. Remove from the heat and let cool completely.

11. Transfer the bulgur to a sieve to drain off any excess liquid (press down on it with a spoon). Transfer the bulgur to a glass or ceramic bowl and add the remaining 4 tablespoons oil, the lemon juice, parsley, mint, tomatoes, and cumin. Toss well to combine. Add the salt and pepper.

12. Preheat the oven to 350°F. Stack the pita bread and wrap it in foil. Place the stack of pita in the oven and heat until warmed through, 10 to 12 minutes.

13. Meanwhile, arrange the stuffed grape leaves, hummus, baba ghanoush, and tabbouleh on each plate. Nestle some green and black olives next to the grape leaves and drizzle some oil on each pile of hummus. Sprinkle the hummus with some paprika.

14. Cut each warmed pita into 8 triangles. Place 4 triangles on each plate and garnish the plates with tomato wedges and some frisée. Serve immediately.

TABBOULEH

5 tablespoons olive oil

⅓ cup fine bulgur

¾ cup boiling-hot water

3 to 4 tablespoons fresh lemon juice

2 cups finely chopped fresh flat-leaf parsley (from 3 bunches)

½ cup finely chopped fresh mint

2 medium tomatoes, seeded and diced

¾ teaspoon ground cumin

¾ teaspoon salt

¼ teaspoon freshly ground black pepper

ASSEMBLY

5 large pita rounds

4 ounces green olives

4 ounces black olives

2 tablespoons extra-virgin olive oil

Sweet paprika

2 medium tomatoes, cut into wedges

10 frisée lettuce leaves

Quick Antipasto

YIELD: 4 SERVINGS

BALSAMIC DRESSING

1 clove garlic, peeled and chopped

Salt and freshly ground black pepper

1 tablespoon balsamic vinegar

2 tablespoons extra-virgin olive oil

ANTIPASTO

1 large eggplant, peeled and
cut into ¼- to ½-inch slices

2 teaspoons salt

4 tablespoons olive oil

8 mushrooms, stemmed

8 thin asparagus spears

6 spinach leaves

4 ounces prosciutto, thinly sliced

4 ounces salami, sliced

1 (6-ounce) jar marinated artichoke
hearts

1 tomato, sliced

8 ounces black olives

8 ounces green Sicilian olives

2 hard-cooked eggs, quartered

1 (2-ounce) can anchovy fillets

4 ounces mild provolone, sliced

1 (6-ounce) jar pimientos or
homemade roasted red peppers
(see page 20)

Coarse salt or sea salt

Breadsticks or warm sliced Italian
bread

Antipasto dishes vary from region to region, depending on the local ingredients available. Quick, basic recipes often include prosciutto, salami, and provolone cheese with marinated vegetables such as artichoke hearts, red bell peppers, and olives (both green and black). When available, incorporate fresh, seasonal ingredients and always try to create an exciting presentation.

1. Make the balsamic dressing: With a mortar and pestle, mash the garlic with a small pinch of salt and pepper. When the garlic is smooth, scrape it into a small bowl and whisk in the vinegar. Very slowly whisk in the oil. Adjust the seasonings. Cover and refrigerate the dressing until ready to use.

2. Make the antipasto: Sprinkle the eggplant slices with the 2 teaspoons salt and place in a colander for 1 hour, to allow excess liquid and any bitter juices to drain.

3. Heat a ridged grill pan over high heat. Rinse the eggplant slices, pat dry well with paper towels, and brush with 1 tablespoon of the oil. Cook in batches for about 5 minutes, turning once, until soft inside and browned on the outside. (Alternatively, grill on a charcoal, electric, or gas grill on an oiled rack over medium heat.) Transfer to a baking sheet and lightly sprinkle with some (not all) of the dressing. Repeat the grilling and marinating process with the mushrooms and the asparagus.

4. Line a large platter with the spinach leaves. Roll the prosciutto slices into loose cylinders and arrange them attractively over the spinach along with the eggplant, mushrooms, asparagus, and all the remaining ingredients except the coarse salt and breadsticks. Serve coarse salt and the remaining balsamic dressing on the side. Accompany with breadsticks.

Prosciutto, Genoa Salami, Melon, Figs, and Olives with Pesto and Balsamic Vinegar

T his composed antipasto teases the palate with a range of flavors and textures on each individual plate (salty, sweet, tangy, bitter, crunchy, and creamy).

Fan 2 slices of cantaloupe on each plate. Twist each slice of salami and prosciutto into a flower shape and arrange on the cantaloupe. Next to the meat add a fig, olive, mozzarella ball, and sun-dried tomato. Just before serving, spoon 1 ½ teaspoons of basil pesto onto the plate and drizzle with 1 teaspoon vinegar. Garnish with the lettuce and basil and serve with a breadstick.

¼ cantaloupe, peeled, seeded, and cut into 8 thin slices

4 thin slices Genoa salami

4 thin slices prosciutto

4 fresh figs or canned Kadota figs

4 green olives

4 frisée lettuce leaves

4 small mozzarella balls (*ciliegine*)

4 moist sun-dried tomatoes packed in oil

2 tablespoons basil pesto, store-bought or homemade

4 teaspoons balsamic vinegar

4 fresh basil sprigs

4 grissini (thin breadsticks)

CHAPTER 8

CREAMY AND BROTHY

Entering the main dining room on board any of our ships, guests are always struck by its elegance and opulence. From the exquisite Rosenthal china and fine linens to the magnificent architecture, antiques, and fine art, the main dining room bespeaks luxury. When guests take their places at the table for one of our five-course meals, they know they are about to partake of a dining experience as rich and well considered as their surroundings—and they are never disappointed.

When I'm creating a new season of menus for the main dining rooms, I'm balancing many factors, so no matter which combinations of courses our guests choose, they will enjoy a highly orchestrated experience of flavors, colors, and textures—while still allowing them to be as adventurous or traditional as their moods and tastes dictate.

The creamy and brothy recipes in this chapter will give you great options for what is classically known as the "soup" course of a five-course meal. This course signals the easing into the meal; the preliminaries and introductions are finished and guests are settling into themselves, the meal, the atmosphere, and the company. The dishes I create for this course in my menus begin by focusing on a texture profile that is always easy and comforting—like soup.

Here you'll find wonderful preparations for sophisticated dishes that include a stew-y ragoût, a creamy risotto, a velvety filled brioche, a melt-in-your-mouth foie gras, two lightly brothy dishes, and, of course, a beautiful bisque. Each small dish is warm and smooth, allowing you to slide deliciously and effortlessly into the next course of your meal.

Seafood Brioche

YIELD: 10 SERVINGS

(See photograph page 5)

SEAFOOD SAUCE

3 tablespoons unsalted butter

3 tablespoons all-purpose flour

3 cups half-and-half

¼ cup medium-dry sherry

½ cup shrimp (or lobster) stock (see Note)

½ teaspoon sweet paprika

Salt

Freshly ground white pepper

This recipe features bay shrimp and bay scallops, which are small enough to leave attractively whole in the mixture. You can substitute larger shrimp and scallops—just chop them after sautéing. The best source for bay shrimp, also called pink shrimp, is Oregon, where they are fished with less damage to the seafloor. They are often sold already cooked and peeled. Diver-caught bay scallops from Mexico are the most sustainably fished bay scallops.

1. Make the seafood sauce: In a large saucepan, melt the butter over medium-high heat. Add the flour and cook, whisking, until bubbly, about 1 minute. Add the half-and-half, sherry, and stock. Bring the mixture to a boil and cook, whisking, until thick and bubbly. Stir in the paprika and season with salt and white pepper.

2. Make the scallops and shrimp: Bring a large pot of salted water to a boil. Prepare a large bowl of ice water. Add the carrots to the boiling water and blanch for 45 seconds. With a strainer, remove the carrots and plunge them into the ice water to stop the cooking. Remove from the ice water and drain on a plate lined with paper towels. Repeat the procedure with the leeks. Set aside.

3. Preheat the oven to 300°F. Place the brioche on a baking sheet and bake until warmed through but not hard, about 10 minutes (3 to 4 minutes if using mini brioches). Remove from the oven and cut the top third from each brioche. Cover with foil to keep warm.

4. Melt 2 tablespoons of the butter in a large skillet over high heat. Add the shallots and garlic and cook, stirring, for 1 minute (do not let the vegetables brown). Add the scallops and sauté until just translucent in the center, about 1 minute. With a slotted spoon, transfer the scallops to a bowl.

5. Add the shrimp to the skillet (if purchased raw) and cook, stirring, for 1 minute. Add the shrimp to the scallops in the bowl.

6. Add the wine to the skillet and bring to a boil. Cook to reduce the liquid, scraping up any browned bits, until about ¼ cup remains in the skillet. Add the seafood sauce and return to a boil slowly over medium heat; stirring, cook until the sauce evenly coats the back of a spoon. Season with salt and white pepper.

7. With a whisk, add 5 tablespoons of the cold butter to the sauce 1 tablespoon at a time, but do not let the sauce return to a boil.

8. Add the shrimp and scallops to the sauce and stir until they are coated. Remove any stray bits of shell or cartilage from the crabmeat, keeping the lumps intact, and gently fold it into the sauce, heating everything until just warmed through. Adjust the seasoning.

9. In a nonstick skillet, heat the remaining 1 tablespoon butter over medium heat. Add the carrots and leeks; sauté until tender and heated through, about 3 minutes; season with salt and white pepper.

10. To serve, place 1 brioche (or 3 mini brioches) on each serving plate. Spoon the seafood mixture into each brioche. Spoon some carrots and leeks onto each brioche and top with the brioche lid. Serve immediately.

SCALLOPS AND SHRIMP

Salt

1¾ cups julienned carrots

1½ cups julienned leeks, white and light green parts only

10 medium-size baked brioche rolls, or 30 mini baked brioches

8 tablespoons (1 stick) cold unsalted butter

½ cup minced shallots

1½ tablespoons minced garlic

¾ pound bay scallops, side muscle removed

1 pound bay shrimp, raw or cooked, peeled

⅔ cup white wine

Freshly ground white pepper

12 ounces jumbo lump crabmeat

NOTE | To make shrimp (or lobster) stock, reserve the shells from 1½ pounds shrimp (or from a 1¼- to 1½-pound lobster that you cooked) and roast them in a small roasting pan at 400°F for about 10 minutes. Put them in a saucepan and fill with water to cover by 1 inch. Add 1 celery stalk, cut to fit into the saucepan, and half an onion, sliced. Place over medium-high heat and when little bubbles rise to the surface, reduce the heat to medium. Never let the liquid boil, and do not stir. Skim off any foam. Cook very gently for about 30 minutes, strain, then return the liquid to the saucepan. Over medium-high heat, cook to reduce the liquid to the amount needed for the recipe.

Foie Gras with Figs, Raspberries, and Balsamic Sauce

Creamy sautéed foie gras is de riguer for an elegant meal, and it's easier to prepare than most people think. Sweet figs and tart raspberries make a perfect counterpoint.

YIELD: 4 SERVINGS

BALSAMIC SAUCE

1 tablespoon seedless raspberry preserves

1 tablespoon balsamic vinegar

1 tablespoon extra-virgin olive oil

Salt and freshly ground black pepper

RASPBERRY PUREE

1 (6-ounce) container fresh raspberries

FOIE GRAS AND FIGS

2 teaspoons plus 2 tablespoons canola oil

3 fresh figs, cut into quarters

1 large shallot, coarsely chopped

Freshly ground black pepper

2 tablespoons port

2 tablespoons red wine

5 fresh thyme sprigs

½ cup chicken stock, good-quality store-bought or homemade

Salt

1 (8-ounce) piece raw Grade A duck foie gras, at room temperature, cleaned and deveined

All-purpose flour, for light dusting

4 thin slices toasted bread, crusts trimmed

4 fresh raspberries

1. Make the balsamic sauce: In a small glass or ceramic bowl, combine the raspberry preserves and vinegar. Push through a sieve into another small bowl. Slowly whisk in the oil. Season with salt and pepper; set aside.

2. Make the raspberry puree: Put the raspberries in a food processor and pulse for 15 seconds, stopping to scrape down the sides. Transfer the raspberry puree to a fine sieve and push it through until mostly seeds are left. Discard the seeds and set the raspberry puree aside.

3. Make the foie gras and figs: In a medium saucepan, heat 2 teaspoons of the oil over medium heat. Add 8 fig quarters (from 2 figs) and the shallot to the saucepan; cook until the figs are slightly caramelized, about 4 minutes. Season with pepper. Add the port, red wine, and 1 thyme sprig and cook to reduce the liquid until it is almost evaporated.

4. Add the stock and cook to reduce the liquid until the sauce evenly coats the back of a spoon, about 8 minutes. Strain the sauce through a fine sieve into a small saucepan and discard the fig quarters. Season with salt and more pepper if needed. Set aside.

5. Cut the foie gras into ½-inch-thick slices and season with salt and pepper. Spread some flour on a plate and lightly dredge the foie gras in it, shaking off the excess.

6. Heat a 10-inch cast-iron skillet over high heat until almost smoking. Brush the skillet with some of the remaining 2 tablespoons oil and add half the foie gras. Cook until golden, 45 to 60 seconds on each side (it will remain pink inside). Quickly transfer the foie gras to a paper towel to drain. Discard the fat in the pan and repeat with the remaining foie gras, but retain 1 tablespoon of fat in the skillet. Add the remaining fig quarters to the skillet, sautéing until tender, about 2 minutes.

7. To serve, divide the toasts among 4 plates and top each with a sautéed foie gras slice. Lay some sautéed fig quarters against the foie gras. Rewarm the fig sauce and spoon it over the figs. Place a spoonful of raspberry puree next to the foie gras and top with a fresh raspberry. Drizzle a little balsamic sauce on each plate and garnish with the remaining thyme sprigs. Serve immediately.

Clams with Pancetta

3 pounds very small (1-inch) hard-shelled clams such as Manila clams

1½ tablespoons olive oil

4 ounces pancetta, chopped

⅔ cup minced shallots

2 cloves garlic, finely minced

1¼ cups fish stock

1 cup white wine

2 pounds tomatoes, peeled, seeded, and chopped (about 1½ cups; see page 111); or 1 cup chopped good-quality canned tomatoes

1½ tablespoons minced fresh parsley

1 teaspoon fresh lemon juice

Salt and freshly ground black pepper

20 slices French bread

4 tablespoons unsalted butter, softened

4 ounces Parmesan cheese, grated

Hungarian paprika

4 medium scallions, white part plus 2 inches green, sliced

Feel free to use larger hard-shelled clams, such as littlenecks (2 to 2½ inches in diameter), but note that the cooking time may increase to 8 to 10 minutes.

1. Scrub the clams well with a brush, discarding any that are dead or have broken shells. Soak the clams in a pot of cold water for a few minutes, drain, then repeat with fresh water 2 or 3 more times until the soaking water stays clear.

2. In a medium stockpot, heat the oil over medium heat. Add the pancetta, shallots, and garlic and cook, stirring, for 4 minutes. Add the stock and wine and bring to a simmer.

3. Gently add the drained clams and the tomatoes. Cover and steam the clams for 2 minutes, shaking the pot occasionally, then begin checking the clams; as soon as they open, use tongs to divide them among 10 shallow bowls. The total steaming time will be 4 to 7 minutes. Discard any clams that do not open. With a slotted spoon, skim the tomatoes and pancetta from the broth and divide them among the bowls.

4. Strain the clam broth through a fine sieve lined with cheesecloth into a saucepan. Bring to a boil over high heat and cook to reduce the liquid by one third. Add the parsley and lemon juice. Season with salt and pepper.

5. Meanwhile, preheat the broiler and lightly toast the bread slices; remove from the oven.

6. In a small bowl, mash together the butter and cheese. Season with paprika, salt, and pepper. Spread the flavored butter onto the toasted bread slices and return them to the oven to melt the butter.

7. To serve, reheat the clam broth and spoon it over the clams in the bowls. Sprinkle with the scallions and serve immediately with the Parmesan toast slices.

Shrimp Wonton and Lemongrass Soup with Bok Choy

YIELD: 6 SERVINGS

SHRIMP WONTONS

12 ounces shell-on shrimp

3 scallions, minced

1 tablespoon minced garlic

1 tablespoon minced fresh cilantro

2 teaspoons minced fresh ginger

3 tablespoons vegetable oil

1½ teaspoons soy sauce

¼ teaspoon salt

36 dumpling or wonton wrappers

1 large egg, lightly beaten with 1 teaspoon water

SOUP

Reserved shells from 12 ounces shrimp

9 cups chicken stock, or 5 (14½-ounce) cans low-salt chicken broth

1 cup finely chopped carrot

⅓ cup very thinly sliced fresh lemongrass (from bottom 5 inches of stalk)

3 tablespoons finely chopped fresh ginger

2 tablespoons minced garlic

1½ ounces dried shiitake mushrooms, soaked in 1 cup cold water for 1 hour

1½ pounds Shanghai bok choy, leaves halved lengthwise, then stalks and leaves thinly sliced crosswise

Salt

Freshly ground white pepper

1½ tablespoons finely chopped fresh basil

1½ tablespoons finely chopped fresh mint

1½ tablespoons finely chopped fresh cilantro

From the menu of our Tamarind restaurant, here's a fragrant lemongrass broth with shrimp wontons, sliced Shanghai bok choy, and a swirl of sesame oil.

1. Make the shrimp wontons: Peel the shrimp and reserve the shells for the soup. Devein the shrimp and finely chop it. In a large bowl, stir together the chopped shrimp, scallions, garlic, cilantro, ginger, oil, soy sauce, and salt.

2. Place a dumpling wrapper on a work surface (keep the remaining wrappers covered with plastic wrap). Spoon a rounded teaspoon of filling into the center of the wrapper and lightly brush the edge of the wrapper with some egg mixture. Lift two opposite corners together to form a triangle and enclose the filling, pressing the edges firmly around the mound of filling to eliminate the air pockets and seal. Moisten the opposite corners of the long side with some egg wash. Curl the moistened corners toward each other, overlapping one on top of the other, and carefully press the corners together to seal (like a tortellini). Repeat with the remaining filling and wrappers.

3. Bring a pot of water to a gentle simmer. Add the wontons in two batches and gently simmer until the filling is just cooked, about 3 minutes per batch. Transfer with a slotted spoon to a platter. Cover to keep warm.

4. Make the soup: In a large pot, combine the shrimp shells, stock, carrot, lemongrass, ginger, and garlic. Bring to a boil over high heat. Reduce the heat and simmer, uncovered, for 20 minutes, stirring and skimming the surface occasionally.

5. Drain the mushrooms, reserving the soaking liquid. Squeeze the mushrooms dry. Cut off and discard the stems. Thinly slice the caps; set aside.

6. Strain the soup into a large bowl, pressing on the solids with the back of a spoon to release as much liquid as possible; discard the solids. Return the soup to the pot and bring to a simmer.

7. Stir in the bok choy, salt, and white pepper; simmer, uncovered, until the bok choy is crisp-tender, 3 to 4 minutes. Add the cooked shrimp wontons, basil, mint, cilantro, chile, and lime juice. Simmer, uncovered, gently stirring, until the wontons are completely heated through, about 2 minutes.

8. Meanwhile, heat the peanut oil in a heavy skillet over high heat. Add the mushrooms and stir-fry for 1 minute.

9. To serve, ladle the soup and wontons into 6 serving bowls and drizzle ½ teaspoon sesame oil over each. With tongs, place some sautéed shiitake mushrooms on the top of each soup. Garnish with the lime slices and serve immediately.

1 small red serrano chile, stemmed and thinly sliced into rounds

1½ teaspoons fresh lime juice

1 tablespoon peanut oil

1 tablespoon toasted sesame oil

6 thin lime slices

French Onion Soup

 f you use a store-bought canned beef broth for this soup, an organic brand will yield the most flavor.

1. In a large soup pot, heat the butter over medium-low heat. Add the onions and cook, stirring gently, until golden brown, about 20 minutes. Stir in the red wine and simmer until the liquid is reduced by half, about 2 minutes.
2. Add the stock and bay leaves and increase the heat to medium-high. Bring to a boil. Reduce the heat to low and simmer, stirring occasionally, for 20 to 25 minutes. Stir in the sherry and season with salt and pepper.
3. Preheat the broiler. Put the baguette slices on a baking sheet and top with the cheese. Toast the bread under the broiler until the cheese is melted. To serve, divide the soup among warmed soup bowls or crocks. Top with the cheese toast and serve immediately.

YIELD: 8 TO 10 SERVINGS

2½ tablespoons unsalted butter

3 pounds onions, thinly sliced

½ cup dry red wine

5½ cups beef stock or low-salt beef broth

2 bay leaves

¾ cup dry sherry

Salt and freshly ground black pepper

8 to 10 slices French baguette

1⅓ cups grated Gruyère cheese (5 ounces)

Curried Coconut Risotto with Shrimp

CURRY COCONUT SAUCE

2 tablespoons vegetable oil

1½ tablespoons curry powder

1½ teaspoons turmeric

¼ teaspoon cayenne pepper

3 cloves garlic, minced

2-inch piece fresh ginger, peeled and minced

1 medium onion, finely diced

Sea salt

½ cinnamon stick

2 cups unsweetened coconut milk

Fresh lime juice

Freshly ground black pepper

RISOTTO AND SHRIMP

1 to 1½ cups vegetable or shrimp stock or water

1 tablespoon olive oil

2 tablespoons unsalted butter

1 cup Arborio rice

¼ cup dry white wine

Sea salt and freshly ground black pepper

1 pound medium shrimp, peeled and deveined

¼ cup chopped roasted cashews

1 pound tomatoes, seeded and chopped

4 fresh cilantro sprigs

ppetizer-friendly shrimp adds little bites of texture to this colorful and coconut-creamy risotto, which celebrates the flavors and aromas of Southeast Asia.

1. Make the coconut-curry sauce: In a medium saucepan, heat the oil over medium heat. Add the curry powder, turmeric, and cayenne pepper and cook, stirring, until toasted, about 1 minute.

2. Add the garlic and ginger and cook, stirring, for 30 seconds. Add the onion and a pinch of salt. Immediately reduce the heat to low and cook, stirring, until the onions are soft and fragrant, about 20 minutes.

3. Add the cinnamon stick and coconut milk and bring to a simmer, scraping up any browned bits from the bottom of the pan. Cook, stirring, for about 20 minutes. Adjust the seasoning and add lime juice and black pepper to taste. Remove from the heat, pour through a fine sieve, and set aside.

4. Make the risotto and shrimp: Bring the stock to a boil in a medium saucepan. Reduce the heat and keep the stock at a low simmer.

5. In a medium enamel-lined cast-iron casserole or other heavy pot, heat the oil and 1 tablespoon of the butter over medium heat. Add the rice and stir with a wooden spoon for about 2 minutes.

6. Add the wine and cook, stirring constantly, until the liquid is absorbed. Add one third of the simmering stock and cook, stirring constantly, until the liquid is absorbed. Add half of the remaining stock and cook, stirring constantly and shaking the pan, until the liquid is absorbed. Add a bit more stock if necessary, so that the risotto is creamy but still slightly firm in the center, about 25 minutes. Season with salt and pepper. Stir in 1 cup of the reserved curry coconut sauce (save the remainder for another purpose) to finish the cooking. Swirl in the remaining 1 tablespoon butter. Adjust the seasoning.

7. Meanwhile, heat a large skillet over medium-high heat until hot. Add the shrimp and season with sea salt and pepper. Cook, stirring occasionally, until the shrimp turn pink and are cooked through, about 3 minutes.

8. To serve, divide the risotto among shallow serving bowls. With tongs, arrange some shrimp on the risotto. Sprinkle the risotto with the cashews and diced tomatoes. Garnish with the cilantro and serve immediately.

Chicken and Mushroom Ragoût in Vol-au-Vent

YIELD: 6 SERVINGS

(See photograph page 8)

VOL-AU-VENT SHELLS

1½ (17.3-ounce) packages frozen puff pastry (3 sheets), thawed

1 large egg, lightly beaten with 1 teaspoon water

CHICKEN RAGOÛT

3 cups chicken stock

1 tablespoon clarified butter (see Note, page 89) plus 3 tablespoons unsalted butter

1 tablespoon all-purpose flour

Salt

Freshly ground white pepper

¾ cup julienned carrots

½ cup julienned leeks, light green parts only

¼ cup minced onion

4 ounces button mushrooms, quartered

1 teaspoon chopped fresh thyme leaves

2 tablespoons dry white wine

¼ cup heavy cream

12 ounces cooked chicken, diced (2½ cups)

¼ cup chopped fresh parsley

6 fresh thyme sprigs

 his recipe is adaptable to different components. Use a matching stock and try it with cooked roasted veal or pork, seafood, even blanched vegetables (pearl onions, peas, carrots, and so on). It's even easier if you purchase pre-made vol-au-vent shells.

1. Make the vol-au-vent shells: Preheat the oven to 400°F. Line one large baking sheet and one smaller baking sheet with parchment paper; set aside. One by one, roll out each puff pastry sheet on a lightly floured surface to ⅛ inch thick (to make a 15-inch by 11-inch rectangle). With a 4-inch round cutter, cut out 6 rounds from each of 2 pastry sheets and 4 rounds from 1 pastry sheet, forming 16 rounds total. Place 8 rounds on the prepared baking sheet; set aside.

2. With a 2½-inch round cutter, cut out smaller rounds from the center of the remaining 8 rounds to make 8 (2 ½-inch) rings. Place the small rounds (for the lids) on the smaller baking sheet. Brush the 4-inch rounds on the larger baking sheet with some beaten egg (be careful not to let the egg run over the edges). Top each round with 1 pastry ring, pressing lightly to adhere, and brush the tops of the rings with some egg mixture (again, be careful not to let the egg run over the edges). Brush the small rounds on the smaller baking sheet with the egg in the same manner.

3. Bake the pastry shells in the center of the oven until golden, about 9 minutes. Transfer the baking sheet to a wire rack to cool. Bake the small rounds (to be the lids) for about 5 minutes; set aside.

4. With a paring knife, carefully cut out and remove the centers from the pastry shells to form cavities. If necessary, return the hollowed-out shells to the oven briefly to dry them out a little. (The pastry shells and lids may be kept, in airtight containers, for up to 2 days. Before filling, reheat them in a 400°F oven until warm.)

5. Make the chicken ragout: Heat the stock to a simmer in a medium saucepan, then lower the heat so that the stock just stays hot. Meanwhile, in a separate heavy saucepan, heat the 1 tablespoon clarified butter over medium-low heat (don't let it turn brown). With a wooden spoon, stir in the flour bit by bit and cook, stirring

constantly, for 2 minutes to remove any raw flour taste (do not let the mixture darken in color). This is the roux.

6. Slowly add the simmering stock a ladleful at a time to the roux, whisking constantly to ensure it's free of lumps. Bring this velouté to a low simmer, stirring frequently, until it has reduced by one third and is smooth and velvety, 20 to 30 minutes. Season the velouté with salt and white pepper and remove from the heat; set aside 1 cup velouté for the ragoût. (The velouté will keep, covered, in the refrigerator for up to 2 days. Gently rewarm before using.)

7. Bring a pot of salted water to a boil. Prepare a large bowl of ice water. Add the carrots to the boiling water and blanch for 45 seconds. With a strainer, remove the carrots and plunge them into the ice water to stop the cooking. Remove from the ice water and drain on a plate lined with paper towels. Repeat the procedure with the leeks. Set aside.

8. Preheat the oven to 350°F. In a large skillet, heat 2 tablespoons of the butter over medium heat. Add the onion and cook, stirring, for 2 minutes (do not let the onion brown). Add the mushrooms and thyme and cook, stirring, until the liquid released from the mushrooms evaporates. Add the wine and cook to reduce the liquid by two thirds. Add the cream and 1 cup velouté; increase the heat to medium-high and bring to a simmer. Reduce the heat and simmer gently until the mixture evenly coats the back of a spoon.

9. Add the chicken and half of the parsley to the cream mixture; cook, stirring, until the chicken is warmed through. Adjust the seasoning.

10. In a nonstick skillet, heat the remaining 1 tablespoon butter over medium heat. Add the carrots and leeks; sauté until tender and heated through, about 3 minutes; season with salt and white pepper.

11. To serve, reheat the vol-au-vent shells and lids in the oven just until warm. Place each shell on a plate (you will have two extra in case of breakage) and spoon in some of the chicken ragoût, with some of the chicken and mushrooms spilling over the side. Spoon some carrots and leeks around the vol-au-vent and place a pastry lid on top at an angle. Garnish with the thyme sprigs and remaining parsley, and serve immediately.

SWEET AND SOUR

One of my greatest pleasures when entertaining is when one of my guests takes their first bite of a dish and says, "Wow!" While every dish needs its own wow factor, I've found that the flavor combinations that surprise the palate are those that immediately receive the almost involuntary exclamations of praise.

The sweet and sour recipes you'll find in this chapter all have the power to surprise and delight your guests with their complex juxtapositions of opposing flavors. Plus, because each one has been designed to ultimately refresh the palate and stimulate the appetite, they make for perfect appetizers.

In addition to the bright flavor interplay, you'll find appetizers that are highly creative, adding unexpected twists to classic concepts. The Fruit-Based Gazpacho—a smoothielike soup that features cantaloupe, pineapple, and bananas with nutmeg and Galliano liqueur—is a dynamite dish that Holland America Line guests absolutely rave over when it makes an appearance on the menu. Replacing a traditional shrimp cocktail with our signature Bay Scallop Cocktail has likewise been a tremendous hit. (For the shrimp lovers in your crowd, the Chile Lime Prawns with Mango Avocado Salsa will be an absolute revelation!)

The range of recipes here is very wise, and you'll be able to find multiple options that will make memorable complements to whatever type of cuisine, theme, season, or menu style you are planning. The Pineapple Boat works equally well for a festive brunch or as part of a formal dinner. The big flavor of the Polenta with Caponata and Crisp Red Onions will make a dynamic start for a main course of prime rib, lamb chops, or any other hearty rustic meal.

When you taste these dishes for yourself, you won't be surprised when your guests begin to rave!

Sliced Orange with Watermelon Salsa

3 cups diced seedless watermelon

½ cup finely diced green bell pepper

2 tablespoons fresh lime juice

2 tablespoons seeded minced jalapeño pepper

1 tablespoon minced fresh cilantro

1 tablespoon minced red onion

½ teaspoon salt

10 navel oranges, peel and pith removed, fruit sliced into rounds

10 fresh mint sprigs

1 cup balsamic vinegar, reduced to ½ cup in a small saucepan over low heat

Watermelon can replace tomato in many dishes. Here, a basic salsa recipe is transformed into salad with watermelon instead of tomato and the sweet/sour interplay between orange and balsamic vinegar.

1. In a glass or ceramic bowl, combine the watermelon, bell pepper, lime juice, jalapeño, cilantro, onion, and salt. Cover and refrigerate for at least 1 hour and up to 3 hours.

2. To serve, overlap orange slices in the center of each plate. Top with a spoonful of watermelon salsa and garnish with the mint sprigs. Drizzle some reduced balsamic around the oranges and serve immediately.

Citrus Compote with Honey and Raisins

T he fruit-salad taste of Gewürztraminer wine, along with its floral aroma, enlivens the marinade of this colorful raw compote.

1. In a glass or ceramic bowl, combine the oranges, grapefruits, kiwis, and raisins. In a separate bowl, stir the Gewürztraminer and simple syrup until mixed. Measure out ½ cup of the Gewürztraminer mixture and pour it over the fruits; gently toss to combine. Cover and refrigerate for at least 1 hour and up to 3 hours.

2. To serve, arrange the fruit in martini glasses and pour the remaining Gewürztraminer mixture over the fruit. Drizzle the honey over the fruit and garnish with the mint sprigs.

YIELD: 10 SERVINGS

10 navel oranges, peel and pith removed, fruit sliced into rounds

5 grapefruits, peel and pith removed, fruit cut into segments

10 kiwi fruits, peeled and sliced

3½ ounces black raisins, soaked in lukewarm water for 30 minutes

1 cup Gewürztraminer wine

½ cup simple syrup (see Note)

⅓ cup honey

10 fresh mint sprigs

NOTE Simple syrup can be made in any quantity you need by combining equal parts sugar and water. If you combine 1 cup water with 1 cup sugar, you will get slightly more simple syrup than is needed for this recipe. The leftovers can be stored for two weeks in the refrigerator or used for drinks (see Cocktails). To make: In a large, heavy pan, combine the sugar and water. Bring to a boil, stirring to dissolve the sugar. Boil for 2 minutes. Remove the pan from the heat and let the syrup cool. Transfer it to a clean bottle or container and chill, covered, until needed.

Pineapple Boat

1 whole pineapple

⅓ cup plus 1 tablespoon sugar

Juice of ½ lemon

Juice of ½ small orange

2 tablespoons green peppercorns

2 tablespoons honey

2 tablespoons chopped fresh cilantro

2½ teaspoons chopped fresh mint, plus 6 whole sprigs for garnish

1 cup flaked coconut, sweetened or unsweetened

6 strawberries, hulled and cut in half

oth sweet and sour, pineapple is the best kind of appetizer: It teases the taste buds and is refreshingly light, so you're primed for the rest of the meal.

1. With a chef's knife, carefully cut the pineapple in half lengthwise, even through the stalk. (Start by putting the knife into the center of the pineapple and cutting through one side first; reposition the knife to cut through the other side.) Then cut each half lengthwise into 3 wedges.

2. With a smaller sharp knife inserted under the fruit and on top of the peel, hollow out each wedge, leaving enough fruit on each peel to maintain its boat shape. Transfer the fruit to a cutting board; set aside. Put the wedges in a container, cover, and refrigerate until ready to use.

3. Trim off any very tough core portions of the pineapple fruit, then cut the fruit into ⅛-inch dice. Put in a glass bowl.

4. In a saucepan, combine 1⅔ cups water, the sugar, lemon juice, orange juice, green peppercorns, honey, cilantro, and chopped mint. Bring to a boil over medium heat, then pour it over the diced pineapple. Gently stir until all the fruit is coated. Let the mixture cool slightly, cover, and refrigerate for 1 day to marinate.

5. Preheat the oven to 350°F. Spread the coconut out in one layer on a baking sheet. Bake, stirring once or twice, for 15 minutes, or until pale golden. Transfer to a bowl and let cool completely.

6. To serve, place a chilled pineapple peel wedge on each plate. With a slotted spoon, arrange some marinated pineapple inside the wedge. Sprinkle with the toasted coconut and garnish with some strawberry halves and a mint sprig and serve.

Bay Scallop Cocktail

Ethereal strands of shaved cucumber add swirling curves and lightness to the look of this flavorful, texture-filled appetizer.

1. Bring the stock to a simmer. Prepare a large bowl of ice water. Add half of the scallops to the simmering stock and blanch for 1 minute. With a strainer, remove the scallops and plunge them into the ice water to stop the cooking. Remove from the ice water and pat dry with paper towels on a plate. Repeat with the remaining scallops.

2. In a glass or ceramic bowl, combine the blanched scallops and lime juice, stirring gently to coat. Season with salt and white pepper. Cover and refrigerate for 2 hours.

3. To serve, divide the shredded lettuce among 10 clear glasses or martini glasses. Top with the cucumber strands and the marinated scallops and lightly drizzle some mustard cognac dressing over. Top with a spoonful of pico de gallo. Garnish with a lime wedge and cilantro sprig and serve.

MUSTARD COGNAC DRESSING

In a glass or ceramic bowl, combine the shallot, vinegar, cognac, mustard, and sugar. Slowly whisk in the oil. Season with salt and pepper. YIELD: ³/₄ CUP

PICO DE GALLO (SALSA FRESCA)

In a glass or ceramic bowl, combine the tomatoes, onion, chiles, cilantro, salt, and pepper. Stir and toss well. Season with lime juice. Let the salsa stand for 2 hours before serving. (The salsa keeps, tightly covered, in the refrigerator for up to 2 days.) YIELD: 2 CUPS

NOTES

- Spiral slicers turn almost any firm vegetable into fine spaghetti-like strands or ribbons. (Look for the Benriner brand.) You can use them to make fried carrot garnishes, potato nests, vegetable spaghetti, or elegant fruit or vegetable salads. If you don't own a spiral slicer, cut matchstick strips or slices with a mandolin.

- Choose firm tomatoes, such as plum tomatoes, rather than soft heirloom varieties for this recipe. There is no need to peel the tomatoes before seeding and dicing.

YIELD: 10 SERVINGS

1½ quarts fish stock

1 pound bay scallops, side muscle removed

1½ tablespoons fresh Key lime juice

Salt

Freshly ground white pepper

2 cups shredded iceberg lettuce

12 ounces English cucumber, peeled and cut into strands with a spiral slicer (see Note)

Mustard Cognac Dressing (recipe follows)

Pico de Gallo (recipe follows)

10 lime wedges

10 fresh cilantro sprigs

MUSTARD COGNAC DRESSING

½ shallot, finely chopped

3 tablespoons red wine vinegar

1 tablespoon cognac

2 teaspoons Dijon mustard

1 teaspoon sugar

⅓ cup extra-virgin olive oil

Salt and freshly ground black pepper

PICO DE GALLO (SALSA FRESCA)

4 medium tomatoes, seeded and diced (see Note)

½ cup finely chopped red onion

2 serrano chiles or jalapeño peppers, seeded and minced

2 to 4 tablespoons chopped fresh cilantro

½ teaspoon salt

Pinch of freshly ground black pepper

1 to 2 tablespoons fresh lime juice

Polenta with Caponata and Crisp Red Onions

YIELD: 4 SERVINGS

(See photograph page 2)

CAPONATA

8 tablespoons olive oil

2 cloves garlic, minced

1 white onion, finely diced

2 tomatoes, seeded and finely diced

1 tablespoon chopped fresh thyme leaves

8 fresh basil leaves, cut into thin strips

Salt and freshly ground black pepper

1 red onion, finely diced

1 zucchini, finely diced

1 yellow squash, finely diced

½ eggplant, finely diced

1 carrot, finely diced

1 red bell pepper, finely diced

1 tablespoon tomato paste

1 tablespoon balsamic vinegar, plus more as needed

POLENTA

1 quart chicken or vegetable stock, store-bought or homemade, or water

1 tablespoon unsalted butter

1 cup coarsely ground cornmeal

2 tablespoons extra-virgin olive oil

¼ cup heavy cream

Salt and freshly ground black pepper

There are many versions of the earthy, sweet-and-sour vegetable stew called caponata, and this one celebrates the fall harvest. Alternatively, caponata can be prepared more traditionally, with olives, celery, and capers replacing the squash, carrots, and bell peppers. You can make this flavorful appetizer completely vegetarian by using water or vegetable stock in the polenta instead of chicken stock.

1. Make the caponata: In a medium skillet, heat 2 tablespoons of the oil over medium-high heat. Add the garlic and white onion and cook, stirring, until the onion just begins to turn golden. Add the tomatoes, thyme, and basil. Bring to a simmer. Cook, stirring, until reduced and thick, 5 to 10 minutes. Season with salt and pepper. Transfer to a large bowl. Set aside.

2. In a clean skillet, heat 1 tablespoon of the oil over medium heat. Add the red onion and cook, stirring, until it just turns golden. Season with salt and pepper. Transfer to the bowl with the tomato mixture. Repeat the procedure with the zucchini, yellow squash, eggplant, carrot, and bell pepper, cooking each separately in 1 tablespoon oil, adding seasoning and then combining with the tomatoes.

3. Transfer all the vegetables to a large skillet. Bring to a simmer over medium-low heat. Add the tomato paste and vinegar and simmer for 20 minutes. Adjust the seasoning, and add more vinegar if desired. Remove from the heat and set aside. (Caponata is best served room temperature or warm, but not hot.)

4. Make the polenta: Butter an 11-by-7-inch baking dish. In a heavy saucepan, bring the stock and butter to a boil over high heat. Slowly whisk in the cornmeal and return to a boil. Reduce the heat to low and simmer, stirring, until the mixture has thickened, 20 to 30 minutes. Whisk in the oil and cream. Season with salt and pepper. Pour into the prepared pan, cover with plastic wrap, and set aside.

5. Make the crisp red onions: In a deep heavy saucepan, heat the oil over medium-high heat until a deep-frying thermometer registers 350°F and the oil is very hot but not smoking (a small piece of bread dropped into the oil should float to the surface almost immediately and brown within 1 minute).

6. Meanwhile, put the flour in a shallow bowl. Season with salt and pepper. Lightly dredge the onion rings in the flour and toss them in a mesh strainer to shake off any excess coating. Deep fry in batches until golden brown, about 2 minutes. Drain on paper towels and keep warm.

7. Brush some oil inside a large round cutter or ring mold. Cut out 4 circles from the polenta (re-oiling the mold between each cut) and place 1 in the center of each plate. Re-oil the mold, position it on 1 of the polenta circles, and fill it to the rim with some caponata, leveling the top. Remove the mold so that a layer of caponata rests flush on top of a layer of polenta. Repeat with the remaining polenta circles and caponata.

8. Lean 2 onion rings on the caponata and encircle with the basil oil and black olive oil. Serve immediately.

BASIL OIL

Bring a large pot of water to a boil. Prepare a large bowl of ice water. Add the basil to the boiling water and blanch for 15 seconds. Remove with a sieve and place in the bowl of ice water to stop the cooking. Drain thoroughly and squeeze dry in a clean kitchen towel. Transfer the basil to a blender. Add the oil and puree until smooth. Transfer the mixture to a fine sieve over a bowl and let the oil drain through into a bowl. The basil oil can be stored, covered, in the refrigerator for up to 3 days. Bring to room temperature before serving. YIELD: ³/₄ CUP

BLACK OLIVE OIL

1. Preheat the oven to 325°F. Pull the papery husks off the garlic head. Slice the tip off of the head to expose the cloves. Rub with a little oil and season with salt and pepper. Place on a square of foil and sprinkle with a bit of water. Pinch the edges of the foil together to enclose the garlic and place on a baking sheet. Roast for 30 to 45 minutes, until very tender. Let cool. Squeeze the garlic flesh from the skin into a small bowl. Measure out 2 tablespoons (save the rest for another use).

2. Transfer the roasted garlic to a blender. Add the olives and oil. Puree until smooth. Transfer to a bowl. The black olive oil can be stored, covered, in the refrigerator for up to 1 day. Bring to room temperature before serving. YIELD: 1¹/₄ CUP

CRISP RED ONIONS

Peanut oil or light olive oil, for frying

½ cup Wondra flour

Salt and freshly ground black pepper

1 large red onion, thinly sliced and separated into rings

BASIL OIL

6 ounces fresh basil leaves

¾ cup vegetable oil

BLACK OLIVE OIL

1 whole head garlic

1 cup extra-virgin olive oil

Salt and freshly ground black pepper

½ cup niçoise olives, pitted

ASSEMBLY

2 tablespoons olive oil

Basil Oil (optional; opposite)

Black Olive Oil (optional; opposite)

Chile Lime Prawns with Mango Avocado Salsa

T hough shrimp and prawns are biologically different creatures (and categorized differently), for this recipe the word *prawn* means simply jumbo shrimp that come 16 or fewer to the pound. As in most cases, in this appetizer large shrimp or prawns can be used interchangeably.

1. Make the mango avocado salsa: In a large glass or ceramic bowl, whisk together the brown sugar and lime juice until the sugar is dissolved. Whisk in the shallot, cilantro, and mint. With a rubber spatula, gently fold in the mangoes and avocado. Set aside.

2. Soak the bamboo skewers (if using) in warm water for at least 30 minutes to prevent charring while cooking.

3. Make the chile lime prawns: In a glass or ceramic bowl, whisk together all the ingredients except the prawns until well combined. Add the prawns, cover, and marinate in the refrigerator for 20 minutes.

4. Remove the prawns from the marinade and thread flat on the skewers, with the skewer going through the prawns at head and tail. (Alternatively, grill without skewers by using a perforated grill pan or by broiling them 3 to 4 inches from the heat element.)

5. Preheat a charcoal, gas, or electric grill to medium-hot (when you can hold your hand 5 inches above the rack for 3 to 4 seconds). Grill the prawns until just cooked through, 2 to 3 minutes on each side.

6. To serve, divide the mango avocado salsa among serving plates and top with the prawns.

YIELD: 4 SERVINGS

MANGO AVOCADO SALSA

2 tablespoons packed dark brown sugar

2 tablespoons fresh lime juice

1 medium shallot, thinly sliced

¼ cup chopped fresh cilantro

2 tablespoons chopped fresh mint

2 firm-ripe mangoes, pitted, peeled, and thinly sliced

½ avocado, chopped

CHILE LIME PRAWNS

10 (6- to 8-inch) metal or bamboo skewers (see Note, page 34)

½ cup olive oil

¼ cup fresh lime juice

3 cloves garlic, minced

2 tablespoons sugar

1 teaspoon ground cumin

½ teaspoon crushed red pepper

1 teaspoon salt

Freshly ground black pepper

1 pound prawns or 16 jumbo shrimp, peeled and deveined (see Note, page 37)

Fruit-Based Gazpacho

YIELD: 3 SERVINGS

½ small cantaloupe

½ pineapple

3 bananas

4 cups vanilla ice cream

4 cups milk

3 tablespoons clover honey

3 pinches freshly grated nutmeg

3 splashes Galliano liqueur

3 splashes medium-dry white wine

 hese fruit-filled Holland America signature soups are creamy-sweet with herb and spice essences from the Galliano liqueur.

1. Cut the cantaloupe, pineapple, and bananas into chunks. One by one in the bowl of a food processor, puree the fruits, separately, until liquidlike in consistency, transferring them to separate glass or ceramic bowls. (Blend the banana as briefly as possible—if browning occurs, the bananas have been overblended.)

2. In the bowl of an electric mixer, mix the ice cream on low speed until soft. Add the milk and blend just until combined.

3. Divide the ice cream mixture among the fruit purees separately and blend with a whisk to an even consistency. Into each bowl, stir 1 tablespoon honey, a pinch of nutmeg, a splash of Galliano, and a splash of wine. Immediately ladle each into 3 chilled glasses or goblets and serve.

CHAPTER 10

COCKTAILS

Holland America Line's full repertoire of fabulous drinks has its own database—so while considering which to choose for this cookbook, the task to select a mere five seemed overwhelming.

What I've done here is provide a short grouping of cocktail recipes that will give you a framework for narrowing down the choices. One good approach is to select an unusual cocktail recipe that has a great story to it. I like this idea not only because it treats your guests to something they likely have never encountered anywhere else but a Holland America Line cruise, but also because it's a great conversation starter.

For example, the Lilikoi is based on an interesting ingredient that's found only in Hawaii and makes an exquisite tropical cocktail. Likewise the Pisco Sour contains pisco, a grape brandy dating back centuries. There's much to discuss!

Another tactic I'll use when selecting a cocktail for an event is to take a look at the hottest restaurant and hotel cocktail lists and spot the latest, chicest cocktail trend. The Juniper Breeze, a gin-based drink flavored with three juices and elderflower cordial, is a good example.

And, finally, I always offer a nonalcoholic cocktail that's as special as any other drink I happen to be featuring and is presented with equal glamour. The Iced Watermelon-Cranberry Drink is refreshing without being overly sweet.

Including an intriguing cocktail on your menu adds a distinctive note of sophistication to the overall dining experience. Start branching out with the cocktail recipes I've included here, and then you can use these strategies to continue to find other great drink recipes that your guests will remember—and talk about—for years to come. Cheers!

Iced Watermelon-Cranberry Drink

YIELD: 4 SERVINGS

1 pound diced seedless watermelon

1 cup cranberry juice

2 cups ice

4 fresh mint sprigs

his pink nonalcoholic drink captures the essence of summer with the sweet, garden-fresh taste of watermelon.

In a blender, combine the watermelon and cranberry juice and pulse until smooth. Transfer the pulp and juice to a fine sieve and strain. Divide the ice among 4 glasses, pour the juice over, and garnish with the mint sprigs.

Juniper Breeze

(See photograph page 13)

YIELD: 1 SERVING

Ice, for shaking and serving

2 ounces Plymouth gin

1½ ounces fresh grapefruit juice

¾ ounce cranberry juice

Splash of fresh lime juice

½ ounce elderflower cordial (available from specialty food stores or online from British foods websites or Amazon)

1 long twist of grapefruit zest

he many different citrus notes help enliven this traditional British combination of gin and elderflower cordial.

Fill glass with ice. Add the gin, juices, and Elderflower Cordial. Cap with shaker can and shake vigorously. Strain over fresh ice into a stemmed glass and garnish with the grapefruit twist.

Lilikoi

T he lilikoi is the variety of passion fruit that's grown in Hawaii. It's yellow, round or oval, and only a few inches in diameter. The combination of passion fruit juice with mango may not replicate the lilikoi taste, but it does evoke the exotic flavors of a tropical paradise.

1. In a blender, puree the mango and passion fruit juice until smooth. Measure out 1 ounce of the mixture and set aside (save the remainder for another use).
2. Fill a shaker glass with ice. Add the tequila, the 1 ounce reserved mango mixture, the liqueur, lime juice, and lemon juice. Cap with the shaker can and shake vigorously. Strain over fresh ice into a stemmed glass.

YIELD: 1 SERVING

1 mango, peeled, pitted, and cut into chunks

⅓ cup passion fruit juice, bottled or diluted from frozen concentrate (available in most Latin American grocery stores)

Ice, for shaking

2 ounces Plata Tequila

1 ounce Marie Brizard Mango Passion liqueur (Grand Marnier can be substituted)

¾ ounce fresh lime juice

¼ ounce fresh lemon juice

Caipirhinia de Uva

(See photograph opposite)

(See photograph opposite)

YIELD: 1 SERVING

3 lime wedges, cut in half

3 green grapes

1 ounce simple syrup (page 151)

Ice

2 ounces Brazilian cachaça

Cachaça is a type of rum from Brazil that isn't made from molasses like other rums but from noncrystallized sugarcane juice—the stage before molasses. (Molasses is produced after crystallization of sugar.) The Caipirhinia is the national cocktail of Brazil. This classic variation adds grapes.

In a shaker glass, hand-press the lime wedges and grapes in the simple syrup with a muddler. Fill the glass with ice. Add the cachaça and cap with the shaker can. Shake vigorously. Pour into a chilled double rocks glass with ice and serve.

Pisco Sour

YIELD: 1 SERVING

1 large egg white (see Note, page 24)

2 ounces Peruvian pisco

¾ ounce simple syrup (page 151)

½ ounce fresh lemon juice

Ice, for shaking

3 drops Angostura bitters

The Spanish settlers in the New World developed pisco—a colorless grape brandy—in the sixteenth century. Whether the Pisco Sour hails from Peru or from Chile is not clear, and has sparked lively debate. On board Holland America Line, we side with Peru.

Put the egg white, pisco, simple syrup, and lemon juice in a shaker glass. Cap with the shaker can and shake vigorously to emulsify the egg white. Add ice and shake again vigorously. Strain into a chilled cocktail glass. Add the Angostura bitters and serve.

APPETIZERS

CHEF'S COUNCIL
RECIPES

As any chef—and the Bible—will tell you, steel sharpens steel.

It was precisely with that thought in mind that I created the Holland America Line Culinary Council. As it takes excellence to improve on what already demonstrates excellence, I formed an elite group of chefs that I consider to be among the most innovative culinary talent on the planet to collaborate with me to keep driving the world-class dining experience at Holland America Line to even greater heights.

The Holland America Line Culinary Council is like a culinary think tank: We evaluate every aspect of our guests' dining experience and brainstorm ways to make it even more memorable. It's exciting to watch this group in action—the creativity and cumulative knowledge in the room when we meet is nothing short of awesome as we imagine new and better ways to impress the guests and deliver the best of the best of what the world of food has to offer—and in the process, we inspire each other.

I'm honored to present this special bonus chapter, which will give you a glimpse of the genius and originality of the Holland America Line Culinary Council, and I have no doubt you will be inspired by what you find in the next few pages. Each recipe is an original signature dish from each chef handpicked for this book and adapted for the home cook.

I encourage you to try every recipe here; they are absolutely fantastic. As you consider which to try first, read through the mini profile of each chef, which will give you some indication of their amazing achievements. You'll undoubtedly cook these imaginative dishes with confidence, knowing you're following the direction of the most celebrated chefs on land and sea.

Tuna Tartare Taco Trio

YIELD: 4 SERVINGS

12 fresh corn tortillas

Peanut oil for frying

1 pound sushi-quality tuna, cut into ¼-inch cubes

4 tablespoons white soy sauce (*shiro shoyu*; see Notes)

1 tablespoon *sambal oelek* (Southeast Asian chile sauce)

1 teaspoon finely grated lime zest

1 teaspoon finely grated lemon zest

4 ounces wasabi *tobiko* (see Notes) or salmon roe

6 medium scallions, white part plus 2 inches green, very thinly sliced lengthwise

From Holland America Line Culinary Council
CHEF DAVID BURKE

Blurring the lines between chef, artist, entrepreneur, and inventor, David Burke stands as one of the leading pioneers in American cooking today. His fascination with ingredients and the art of the meal has fueled a career marked by creativity, critical acclaim, and the introduction of revolutionary products and cooking techniques. In addition to David Burke Townhouse (New York City), Burke's other properties include Fishtail by David Burke and David Burke at Bloomingdale's (both also in New York), Burke in the Box at McCarran Airport (Las Vegas), David Burke's Primehouse (Chicago), David Burke Fromagerie (Rumson, New Jersey), David Burke Prime (Mashantucket, Connecticut), and David Burke Kitchen in the James Hotel (New York City).

1. With a wide-mouth coffee mug or a lid as a template, cut a 3-inch circle from each tortilla. In a 12-inch cast-iron skillet or wok, heat 2 inches of oil over medium-high heat until a deep-frying thermometer registers 325°F. Line a wire rack with paper towels.

2. Use a pair of tongs to grasp one edge of a tortilla circle. Transfer the tortilla to the hot oil and use the tongs to bend it into a taco-shell shape (you can hold the tortilla in place by pushing it against the side of the skillet with a large spoon). When one side of the tortilla is crisp and slightly golden, switch sides with the tongs to repeat the process until both sides are fried. Transfer the taco shell to the wire rack and repeat with the remaining tortilla circles. Set aside.

3. Combine the tuna, soy sauce, *sambal oelek*, and lime and lemon zests in a stainless-steel bowl sitting in a larger bowl of ice. With a rubber spatula, gently fold the mixture until combined.

4. To serve, place a spoonful of the tuna mixture into each crisp taco shell. Top each with 1 teaspoon *tobiko* and 1 tablespoon sliced scallions. Serve 3 tacos per plate.

NOTES

- White soy sauce (*shiro shoyu*) has a lighter color than most soy sauces because it's fermented for a shorter amount of time, and has a mellower aroma and delicate flavor. It contains a higher percentage of wheat compared to other soy sauces.

- *Tobiko* is flying-fish roe. Wasabi *tobiko* is *tobiko* that's been flavored with wasabi, which is the Japanese equivalent of horseradish. The vibrant green wasabi *tobiko* is very spicy to the tongue and should be used to taste. Wasabi *tobiko* is available at some specialty foods shops and by mail order online.

Salmon Tartare with Cucumber Juice and Curry Cream

(See photograph page 182)

CUCUMBER JUICE

1 large or 2 medium cucumbers, peeled and trimmed and put through a juicer (or pureed in a food processor and pushed through a fine sieve) to yield a scant ¾ cup juice

3 tablespoons finely chopped shallot

1 large clove garlic, finely minced

1 teaspoon distilled white vinegar

1 teaspoon sushi vinegar (see Notes)

¼ teaspoon salt

⅛ to ¼ teaspoon xanthan gum (see Notes)

CURRY CREAM

½ slice bacon, diced

1¾ teaspoons curry powder

1½ teaspoons chopped fresh thyme

1½ teaspoons chopped fresh rosemary

1 large clove garlic, minced

7 tablespoons sunflower oil

1 teaspoon frozen egg white

1 teaspoon sushi vinegar (see Notes)

1½ tablespoons plain Greek yogurt

¼ teaspoon salt

1 teaspoon fresh lemon juice

From Holland America Line Culinary Council
CHEF JONNIE BOER

Jonnie Boer is head chef at De Librije in Zwolle, Netherlands, recognized as one of the fifty best restaurants in the world by *Restaurant* magazine and only the second restaurant in the Netherlands to be awarded three Michelin stars. His catering company, Food on Tour, sells its own products, and in 2008 Boer and his wife, Thérèse, opened a new hotel with restaurant, as well as a cooking and wine school. The restaurant, Librije's Zusje, was awarded its first Michelin star within six months of opening. Boer was named a Knight in the Order of Orange Nassau in 2005, one of the Netherlands' highest honors.

1. Make the cucumber juice: In a glass or ceramic bowl, combine the cucumber juice, shallot, and garlic. Allow the flavors to blend for 1 hour.
2. Strain the mixture through a fine sieve into a blender and add the white vinegar, sushi vinegar, and salt. Put on the lid (remove the filler cap), and blend the mixture while slowly adding the xanthan gum through the center of the lid, adding only enough xanthan gum to create a thickened sauce. Transfer to a glass bowl, cover, and refrigerate until needed.
3. Make the curry cream: In a skillet, heat the bacon very slowly over medium-low heat, stirring occasionally, so that the bacon fat melts and the flavor of the bacon is released, about 20 minutes. Stir in the curry powder and then the thyme, rosemary, and garlic. Add the oil and heat without browning for 3 minutes, to allow the flavors to infuse the oil. Strain the contents of the skillet through a fine sieve into a bowl. Season with the salt and lemon juice. Let cool to room temperature.

4. In a blender, combine the egg white and vinegar. Put on the lid (remove the filler cap) and blend on the lowest setting for 2 seconds. While blending, add the curry-infused oil very slowly through the center of the lid until the mixture is emulsified and resembles mayonnaise. Transfer to a glass bowl and gently whisk in the yogurt just until combined. Cover and refrigerate until needed.

5. Make the salmon tartare: With a chef's knife, very finely mince the salmon and place in a glass or ceramic bowl. Add the shallot, crème fraîche, lime juice, and salt. With a rubber spatula, gently fold the mixture until combined. On a piece of parchment paper, spread the mixture into several compact strips that are about 1¼ inches wide and ¾ inch tall. Cover with plastic wrap and chill for at least 1 hour and up to 4 hours.

6. To serve, use a 1-inch circular cutter to cut out cylinders from the salmon strips. With a small metal offset spatula, lift and place 3 to 5 cylinders of salmon tartare on each chilled serving plate. (Alternatively, use a small cookie scoop to make small, rounded mounds of tartare.) Surround the salmon with dots of curry cream. Garnish each plate with 2 cherry tomato halves and 2 cornichon halves. Roll the zucchini strips into cylinders and place 3 or 4 on each plate. Drizzle the plates with the cucumber juice and garnish with the watercress, frisée, and chives. Serve immediately.

NOTES

- To make sushi vinegar, in a small saucepan combine ¼ cup unseasoned rice vinegar, 1 tablespoon sugar, 1½ teaspoons of mirin or sake, and 1½ teaspoons salt. Heat over low heat, stirring, until the sugar and salt have dissolved.

- Xanthan gum is a commercial thickener that is often available in stores carrying gluten-free cooking and baking ingredients. It helps create a suspension of ingredients, but unlike gelatin it is completely vegan. To thicken sauces with xanthan gum, start by sprinkling about ⅛ teaspoon per 1 cup of liquid in a blender and blend immediately so it doesn't form clumps.

SALMON TARTARE

8 ounces skinless salmon fillet, preferably wild

2 tablespoons minced shallot

1½ tablespoons crème fraîche

1½ teaspoons fresh lime juice

¼ teaspoon salt

10 cherry tomatoes, cut in half

10 cornichons, cut in half lengthwise

3½ ounces baby zucchini (about 8), trimmed and thinly sliced in lengthwise strips with a mandoline (page 70)

1 ounce watercress (¼ bunch)

1 ounce frisée lettuce

30 fresh chives

Corn Pancakes with Chili-Covered Gravlax

Adapted from New American Table by Marcus Samuelsson

YIELD: 8 SERVINGS

CHILI-COVERED GRAVLAX

1 cup sea salt

1 tablespoon fennel seeds

2 cups light brown sugar

½ cup mild chili powder

1½ pounds skin-on salmon fillet, in one piece, pin bones removed

5 fresh cilantro sprigs, roughly chopped

2 (3-inch) pieces ginger, peeled and grated

CORN PANCAKES

¼ cup yellow cornmeal

¼ cup blue cornmeal

3 tablespoons all-purpose flour

½ teaspoon salt

½ teaspoon mild chili powder

¼ cup sour cream

½ cup heavy cream

1 large egg

½ cup cooked corn (from 1 cob), chopped

2 scallions, white and light green parts only, minced

4 drops of Tabasco sauce

3 tablespoons corn oil

Fresh cilantro sprigs

From Holland America Line Culinary Council
CHEF MARCUS SAMUELSSON

Marcus Samuelsson's recipes are inspired by spices, color, and local fresh ingredients. Born in Ethiopia, Samuelsson grew up in Sweden with his adoptive parents. His adoptive grandmother taught him to cook, and he's now the proprietor of the popular Harlem, New York, restaurant Red Rooster. His best-selling *New American Table* cookbook celebrates local farms and kitchens. He is the winner of Bravo's *Top Chef Masters* (season 2) and was guest chef at the White House for the Obama administration's first state dinner for Prime Minister Singh of India. In addition to Red Rooster, Samuelsson's other properties include Marc Burger in Macy's (Chicago, and Costa Mesa, California), the fast-casual Street Food (Stockholm), and C-House, a New American seafood-and-chophouse in the Affinia Chicago hotel.

1. Make the chili-covered gravlax: In a small bowl, combine the salt, fennel, sugar, and chili powder, mixing well. Put the salmon in a shallow dish and rub a handful of the salt mixture into both sides of the fish. Sprinkle the salmon with the remaining mixture and cover with the cilantro and ginger. Cover with plastic wrap and let stand for 3 hours at room temperature.

2. Transfer the salmon to the refrigerator and let cure for 12 hours.

3. Scrape the seasonings off the salmon. Thinly slice the salmon on the bias.

4. Make the corn pancakes: Preheat the oven to 200°F. In a medium bowl, whisk the yellow and blue cornmeals, flour, salt, and chili powder. In a larger bowl, whisk the sour cream, heavy cream, egg, corn, scallions, and Tabasco sauce until combined. Add the cornmeal mixture and whisk until just combined.

5. In a nonstick skillet, heat 1 tablespoon of the oil over medium heat.
   Working in batches, pour 1 tablespoon of the batter for each pancake
   onto the hot skillet and cook until bubbles appear on the surface
   and the bottom is golden, about 2 minutes. Turn with a spatula
   and cook for another 2 minutes. With a slotted spoon, remove the
   pancakes to a baking sheet. Keep the finished pancakes warm in the
   oven while you cook the remaining pancakes in batches, adding the
   remaining 2 tablespoons oil to the pan if necessary.

6. To serve, place 2 or 3 corn pancakes on each serving plate and top
   with a slice of chili-cured salmon. Garnish with the cilantro and
   serve immediately.

Tai Snapper Carpaccio with Blood Orange Juice, Extra-Virgin Olive Oil, and Lemon Thyme

YIELD: 4 SERVINGS

(See photograph page 12)

1¼ pounds blood oranges

½ cup extra-virgin olive oil

2 fennel bulbs (about 1¾ pounds total), stalks cut off and discarded

1 small tai snapper, cleaned, filleted, skin removed, pin bones removed (see Note)

Fleur de sel or sea salt

Freshly ground grains of paradise (see Notes)

Pinch of fennel pollen (see Notes)

4 fresh lemon thyme sprigs

From Holland America Line Culinary Council
CHEF CHARLIE TROTTER

Charlie Trotter is the chef of a Chicago restaurant that bears his name. Charlie Trotter's has won ten James Beard Foundation awards, is a member of the prestigious Les Grandes Tables du Monde, and is a Mobil five-star restaurant. *Wine Spectator* named the restaurant "The Best Restaurant in the World for Wine & Food" (1998) and "America's Best Restaurant" (2000). Chef Trotter has written fourteen cookbooks and three management books and is the host of the nationally aired, award-winning PBS cooking series *The Kitchen Sessions with Charlie Trotter*. In addition to his namesake restaurant, Chef Trotter owns and operates Trotter's To Go, a gourmet retail shop in the Lincoln Park neighborhood of Chicago, and also produces a line of organic-based food products. Recognized as Humanitarian of the Year by the International Association of Culinary Professionals, Trotter's foundation raises money to support people seeking careers in the culinary arts.

1. With a sharp knife, trim the top and bottom off 1 of the oranges. Stand the orange upright and cut downward to remove the rind and pith in thick strips. Working over a bowl, cut between the membranes to release the segments. Pour any juice from the oranges into a 1-cup measuring cup; set the orange segments aside.

2. Add enough juice from additional oranges to make ½ cup juice. Pour ¼ cup juice into a small glass bowl and whisk in 3 tablespoons of the oil. Add the orange segments and gently toss to coat; set aside to marinate for 15 minutes.

3. Quarter the fennel bulbs lengthwise and cut out and discard most of the cores, leaving just enough core to keep the portions of fennel intact. With a mandoline slicer, cut the fennel lengthwise into paper-thin slices (see Note, page 70).

4. Pour the remaining ¼ cup juice into a small glass bowl and whisk in 2 tablespoons of the oil. Add ½ cup of the fennel slices and gently toss to coat; season with salt. (Save the remaining fennel for another use.)

5. Cut the fish into 12 thin slices that are 4 inches long by 2 inches wide. Season the slices with salt and grains of paradise. Rub with 3 tablespoons of the oil.

6. To serve, arrange 3 slices of the marinated snapper in the center of each plate and put a mound of marinated fennel alongside. Place a few pieces of the marinated orange segments around the snapper and dress with the 2 tablespoons of the liquid from the oranges. Sprinkle fennel pollen on and around the snapper and grind some grains of paradise over the plate. Garnish with lemon thyme and serve immediately.

NOTES

- Red snapper is known as "tai" when prepared for sushi.

- Grains of paradise are peppery, aromatic seeds from West Africa. Grind them in a pepper mill for this recipe.

- Fennel pollen is the pollen from fennel flowers; it has a sweet and intensely fennel flavor (a little goes a long way). Both of these spices are available online from thespicehouse.com or from specialty food markets.

Grilled Crostini with Chocolate and Orange Zest

1 good-quality baguette, cut slightly on the diagonal into ⅓-inch-thick slices

⅓ cup extra-virgin olive oil

1 (3.5-ounce) bar 70% cacao bittersweet chocolate

1½ tablespoons flaked sea salt, such as Maldon

2 tablespoons very thin strips orange zest

From Holland America Line Culinary Council
CHEF JACQUES TORRES

One of the world's most respected chocolatiers and pastry chefs, Jacques Torres is the executive officer of Jacques Torres Chocolate, producing and selling his hand-crafted chocolates and confectionery products at factory and retail locations in New York City and at Atlantic City's Harrah's Casino. Torres has served as executive pastry chef at Le Cirque, winning awards, judging competitions, and participating in culinary events. He hosted *Dessert Circus with Jacques Torres* on television, and produced the books *Dessert Circus: Extraordinary Desserts You Can Make at Home* and *Dessert Circus at Home*. He also hosted *Chocolate with Jacques Torres* on the Food Network.

1. Preheat a charcoal, gas, or electric grill to medium-hot (when you can hold your hand 5 inches above the rack for 3 to 4 seconds). Grill the bread slices for 1 to 2 minutes on each side, until pale golden and lightly marked but not burned.

2. Preheat the oven to 200°F. Place the bread slices concave side up on a baking sheet and drizzle with the oil. Break the chocolate into shards and press a shard into each bread slice. Bake just until the chocolate softens, 2 to 3 minutes. Remove from the oven (do not spread the chocolate) and sprinkle with the salt and some orange zest. Serve immediately.

ACKNOWLEDGMENTS

So many talented people had a hand in making this
beautiful book about beginnings possible.

First, I'd like to honor the members of the Holland America Line Culinary Council. It is a great privilege to work so closely with Jonnie Boer, David Burke, Marcus Samuelsson, Charlie Trotter, and Jacques Torres on the ongoing development of Holland America Line culinary programs. I thank them specifically for the contribution of their signature recipes for publication in this book, and special thanks to Chef Trotter for penning the foreword to this book. His unique culinary vision and perspective on life and food always provide brilliant food for thought.

Just as great meals begin first in the imagination, the realization of great projects begins first in the vision of leadership. The insight and boldness of the Holland America Line leadership team is without parallel, and I'd like to acknowledge the continuing commitment to culinary excellence of Stein Kruse, President and Chief Executive Officer; Rick Meadows, President Seabourn Cruises and Executive Vice President, Holland America Line; Dan Grausz, Executive Vice President, Fleet Operations; Johan Groothuizen, Vice President, Marine Hotel Operations; and Judy Palmer, Vice President, Marketing Communications.

In particular, I'd like to tip my toque to Dan Grausz, Executive Vice President of Fleet Operations, who is one of the hardest working people I have ever met—and that's saying something in an organization comprised entirely of committed human beings. Dan, I cannot thank you enough for all you and Johan do for Holland America Line, its guests, and most especially for the constant support you've given my culinary vision and for the personal encouragement!

In fact, it is truly thanks to Dan Grausz and Johan Groothuizen, Vice President, that you now hold this beautiful book in your hands. Like Dan, Johan has been an enthusiastic supporter of my quest to put Holland America Line's signature recipes Culinary Signature Collection into the kitchens of our guests. Starting with the first in this popular series of cookbooks, the first-ever Holland America Line cookbook *A Taste of Excellence* (Rizzoli, 2006), Johan and Dan have been a continual source of inspiration and encouragement in producing these books, of which *Appetizers* is now the fourth. Thanks to their leadership, you can begin looking ahead to the fifth volume, *Desserts*, which has already begun production.

I'd also like to thank each and every member of the Holland America Line Culinary and the Marine Hotel departments for the great work they do ensuring that every ingredient, every dish, every detail of culinary operations is executed with excellence—and while my name goes on the cover of the menus and books, without their unfailing commitment to the work they do, our culinary offerings would not continue to garner the accolades they enjoy.

For testing and retesting the final recipes so they are appropriate for the home chef, I am extremely thankful for Holland America Line's Corporate Executive Chef, John Mulvaney, who travels with his chefs on the fleet and ensures that all new dishes are implemented correctly and that the cooking and presentation specifications I created for our menus are adhered to.

In addition, I'd like to acknowledge the ongoing efforts of Steve Kirsch, Director Culinary; John Peijs, Deputy Director Hotel Marine Operations; Orion Balliet, Fleet Executive Chef; Troy Wastell, Senior Executive Chef Operations; Jonathan Ben-Ammi, Culinary Operations Administrator; and Natalie Paige, Purchasing Manager. I also truly appreciate the work of our executive chefs, who tirelessly test and retest the recipes with Orion and John.

I never cease to be amazed at the endless range of talent demonstrated by what I think of as my special cookbook tactical team—over so many years and so many magnificent, well-received publications; we've developed clockwork-like precision. It starts with Monica Velgos, who works with me on the recipes and adapts them for use for the home cook. Next, my wonderful professional photographers Herb Schmitz and Pat Doyle bring their brilliant passion to the signature style photography that illustrates each edition in such bright and exquisite detail. Herb has been a good enough teacher over the last three decades doing the photos for twelve cookbooks that I can now add professional food photography to my own roster of skills!

While on the topic of photography, I'd like to take a moment to thank the people who provide the beautiful tableware you'll see in these pages: Sarah Mowat, USA Marketing Executive, Churchill, Inc.; Claude Peiffer, Managing Director, RAK Porcelain Europe; Anne Valette, North American Sales Manager, Revol USA; Kurt Newman, Regional Sales Manager, Steelite International; and Andrea Vianello, Chief Executive Officer, Rosenthal USA.

Once the photography is complete, my gifted writer Marcelle Langan takes over and works with me to craft the words that define my thoughts for the copy in the book.

On a personal note, I enjoy a truly adventurous culinary life that involves traveling the world over. While exciting, it does not in any way leave me with anything like what one could consider a typical schedule. It takes a very special effort indeed to maintain quality, long-term relationships with someone who jets in and out as frequently as I do. Yet, my life has been blessed with some wonderful people who I am so proud to call my friends—Zane Tankel, Sigrid and Klaus Reisch, Fran Scott, Sirio Maccioni, and Michael Smith. I thank you for your steadfast loyalty and for your friendship.

My deepest thanks and appreciation are always reserved for my children: Magnus, Kenneth, and Kristina. The pride I take in you fills me with energy and inspiration for everything else I do in life. Watching you all grow and begin to discover and cultivate your own passions are my greatest joys; being your father my greatest honor.

And, last, but never least, to all of you readers who will choose to start your party with a recipe from *Appetizers*, I raise my glass and offer this toast: I wish you a perfect recipe of success and joy whenever you take the time to create a meal for your family and friends.

On behalf of myself and Holland America Line, we are honored that with this book, the Holland America Line family comes into your home for you to share with yours.

Cheers!
RUDI SODAMIN
Master Chef, Holland America Line

CONVERSION TABLES

THE TABLES BELOW ARE APPROXIMATE

WEIGHTS

AMERICAN	METRIC
⅛ ounce	3.5 grams
¼ ounce	7.5–8 grams
½ ounce	15 grams
¾ ounce	20 grams
1 ounce	30 grams
2 ounces	55 grams
3 ounces	85 grams
4 ounces (¼ pound)	110 grams
5 ounces	140 grams
6 ounces	170 grams
7 ounces	200 grams
8 ounces (½ pound)	225 grams
9 ounces	255 grams
10 ounces	285 grams
11 ounces	310 grams
12 ounces (¾ pound)	340 grams
13 ounces	370 grams
14 ounces	400 grams
15 ounces	425 grams
16 ounces (1 pound)	450 grams
1¼ pounds	560 grams
1½ pounds	675 grams
2 pounds	900 grams
3 pounds	1.35 kilos
4 pounds	1.8 kilos
5 pounds	2.3 kilos
6 pounds	2.7 kilos
7 pounds	3.2 kilos
8 pounds	3.4 kilos
9 pounds	4.0 kilos
10 pounds	4.5 kilos

TEMPERATURES

FAHRENHEIT	CELSIUS	GAS MARK
40	4.5	
50	10	
65	18	
105	41	
115	46	
120	49	
125	52	
130	54	
135	57	
150	70	
175	80	
200	100	0
225	110	¼
250	130	½
275	140	1
300	150	2
325	170	3
350	180	4
375	190	5
400	200	6
425	220	7
450	230	8
475	240	9
500	250	
525	270	
550	290	

LIQUID MEASURES

	FLUID OUNCES	MILLILITER
¼ cup	3	60
⅓ cup	4	80
½ cup	6¼	120
1 cup	12.5	240
1 pint (2 cups)	20	570
¾ pint	15	425
½ pint	10	290
⅓ pint	6.6	190
¼ pint	5	150
1 quart	50	960
1 gallon	200	3.84 liters
2 scant tablespoons	1	28
1 tablespoon	½	15
1 teaspoon	–	5
½ teaspoon	–	2.5
¼ teaspoon	–	1.25

LENGTHS

AMERICAN	METRIC
¼ inch	6 millimeters
½ inch	12 millimeters
1 inch	2½ centimeters
2 inches	5 centimeters
4 inches	10 centimeters
6 inches	15 centimeters
8 inches	20 centimeters
10 inches	25 centimeters
12 inches	30 centimeters
14 inches	35 centimeters
16 inches	40 centimeters
18 inches	45 centimeters

APPROXIMATE AMERICAN/METRIC CONVERSIONS

ITEM	AMERICAN	METRIC
Flour	1 cup / 4¼ ounces	115 grams
Granulated sugar	1 cup / 7 ounces	200 grams
Brown sugar (packed)	1 cup / 8 ounces	225 grams
Brown sugar (packed)	1 tablespoon / ½ ounce	15 grams
Butter	1 cup / 8 ounces	225 grams
Raisins (loose)	1 cup / 5¼ ounces	145 grams
Uncooked rice	1 cup / 7 ounces	200 grams
Cocoa powder	¼ cup / ¾ ounce	20 grams

INDEX